Holiday Woodworking Projects

90 Patterns for Festive Decorations

JOYCE AND JOHN NELSON

STACKPOLE
BOOKS

Copyright © 1993 by Stackpole Books

Published by
STACKPOLE BOOKS
5067 Ritter Road
Mechanicsburg, PA 17055

Printed in the United States of America

First Edition

10 9 8 7 6 5 4 3 2 1

Library of Congress Cataloging-in-Publication Data

Nelson, Joyce C.
    Holiday woodworking projects : 90 patterns for festive decorations /
Joyce Nelson and John Nelson. — 1st ed.
        p.   cm.
    ISBN 0-8117-2547-2
    1. Woodwork. 2. Holiday decorations. I. Nelson, John A., 1935–.
II. Title.
TT180.N48   1993
745.594'1—dc20   93-17075
                                                                CIP

CONTENTS

Introduction

The holidays are important to everyone, especially families. These days, you can purchase all kinds of holiday decorations, but they cannot match the warmth and pride that come with making your own and giving them to family and friends.

Many home-crafted decorations will be used year after year and perhaps be handed down from generation to generation, so it is important to sign and date them. Otherwise, you will soon forget when you started using a particular project. We have tried to present these projects so that anyone with limited tools and experience can complete them. None has to be made, painted, or stained exactly as shown and surely none has to be perfect. In fact, it really makes it your own if you use your imagination.

On most of the projects, I used an artist acrylic paint. On projects that required them, I used hobby craft quick-drying enamel metallic brass, metallic chrome, and metallic bronze paints. They can be found in most craft or hardware stores.

The projects may be enlarged or reduced to whatever size you need. All can be made with hand tools or power tools, though a few power tools can speed things up. One power tool I would recommend would be a power scroll saw, which ranges from $300 to $1,800. Such saws are safe as long as you use precautions and respect them as you would any machine. They also are quiet and easy to use.

John and I hope you will have many hours of pleasure making these holiday projects and that you, your family, and friends will enjoy them for years to come. We welcome suggestions or comments.

Selecting Materials and Supplies

Many of the smaller items can be made of scrap wood from other projects. Even if you purchase wood, the overall cost for materials is very low, but it really pays to buy the best wood you can find. Grade A pine without knots or high-grade plywood without voids will make your work easier, make your finished projects look better, and probably save you time. Suppliers are in the Appendix. Write for their catalogs, which offer ideas for even more projects. For example, you could add a music box feature with a special tune to personalize a project as a gift for someone special. Again, this book is only a guide for your own ideas.

Enlarging or Reducing a Pattern

Most of the patterns are full size in order to make your job easier, but you can make them any size you wish. There are four ways to enlarge or reduce a pattern. One of the simplest is to reproduce it on a photocopier that enlarges or reduces images. For extreme changes, reduce the reduction (or enlarge the enlargement) until you get the size you want.

Another good method is to get a photomechanical transfer of the design made at a printing shop. This is easy and the cost ($5 to $15, depending on the size) is worth it if your time is valuable.

The third method is to use a pantograph, a drawing tool whose adjustable arms can enlarge or reduce a drawing to most any size. If you do a lot of enlarging or reducing, this tool may be well worth its modest price ($5 to $15).

However, the method most often used by woodworkers is the "grid and dot-to-dot" technique. It is simple, doesn't require artistic skills, and can be used to enlarge or reduce to any size or scale. A ruler, T square, 45-degree triangle, and masking tape help, but you can use what you have at home. Follow these steps to adapt pattern sizes.

1. Make a copy of the original pattern and draw a grid over it. The size of the original grid often depends on the intricacy of the original pattern. In Figure 1, we've used an original grid of 1/8 inch. For a less detailed pattern, we might have selected a larger original grid. Now decide on the size you want for the finished project. For a final size twice as large as the original, use a grid twice as big as the original grid, or 1/4 inch.

2. Starting from the upper left corner, letter each column on the original grid. From the same starting point, number the rows to the bottom. In this example, the columns run from A through R and the rows from 1 through 28.

3. Tape a blank sheet of paper to a drafting board and carefully draw the final grid, using the same number of columns and rows.

4. On your final grid, mark columns and rows the same way.

5. On the original, mark dots along the pattern outline wherever it crosses a line.

6. On your final grid, carefully draw dots corresponding to the ones you marked on the original. The numbers and letters guide you.

7. Connect the dots. You do not have to be exact; simply sketch lines between them.

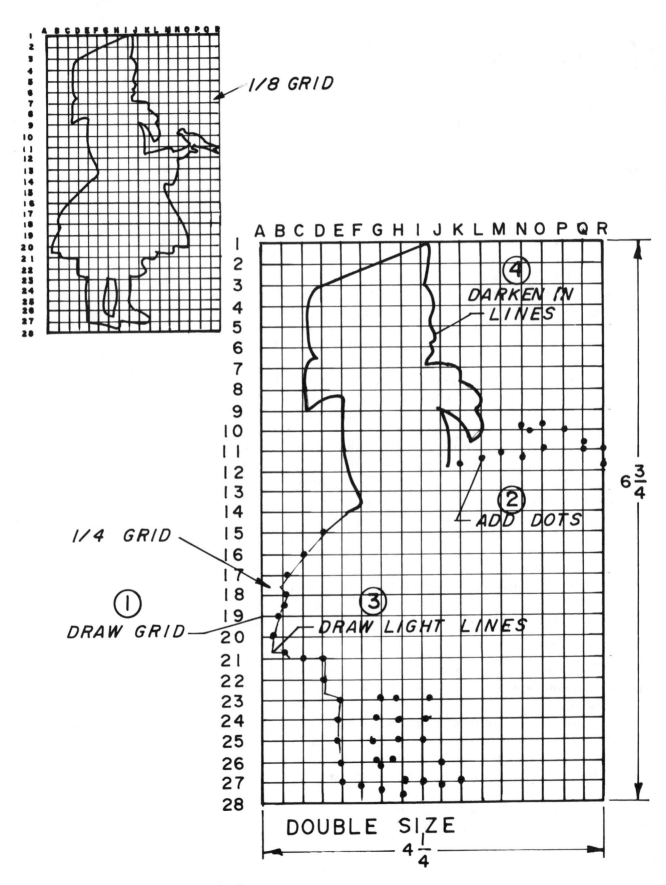

1/8 GRID

A B C D E F G H I J K L M N O P Q R

④ DARKEN IN
LINES

1/4 GRID

① DRAW GRID

② ADD DOTS

③ DRAW LIGHT LINES

6 3/4

DOUBLE SIZE

4 1/4

4

Transferring the Pattern from Paper to Wood

Before transferring the pattern, sand the surfaces of the wood until they are very smooth. You will be able to see the pattern much better and your piece will move around the tabletop more easily. Then note the direction of the grain. Place your pattern on the wood so that any extended features, such as an animal's legs or tail, are parallel to the grain. The narrow areas may break off if you don't position the grain carefully. Sometimes features go both ways, so you may have to place the pattern diagonal to the grain.

There is a quick, clean method for transferring a pattern ($8\frac{1}{2}$ by 11 inches or smaller) to a piece of wood. Photocopy the pattern, then tape the copy, printed side down, to the wood. Using a hot flat iron or woodburning set, heat the back side of the copy; the pattern will be transferred directly to the wood.

You can also take a photocopy and affix it directly to the wood with rubber cement. You will then have a clean, sharp image of the

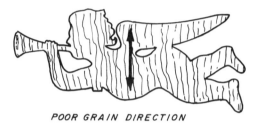

POOR GRAIN DIRECTION

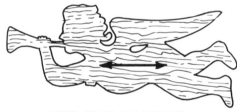

BEST GRAIN DIRECTION

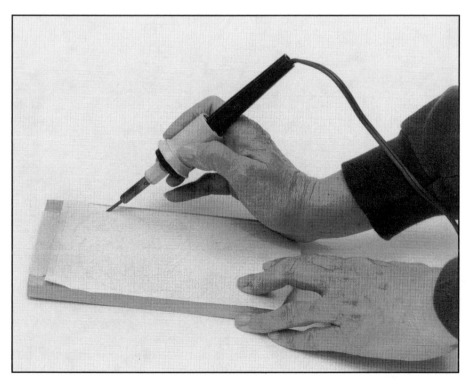

5

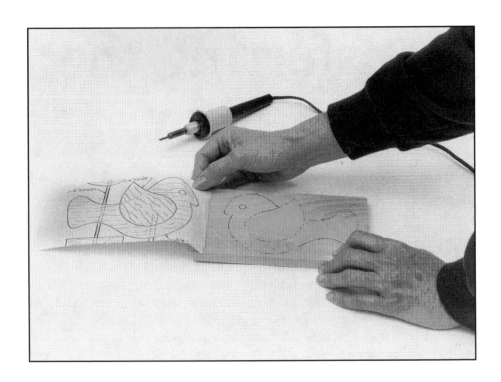

pattern. The paper can be easily removed after you make the cuts. I especially like this method.

Another quick method is to place a sheet of carbon paper between the pattern and the wood and trace the lines. This works well for patterns larger than 8½ by 11 inches, but you'll need large sheets of carbon paper. Meisel Hardware Specialties sells 17-by-22-inch sheets of

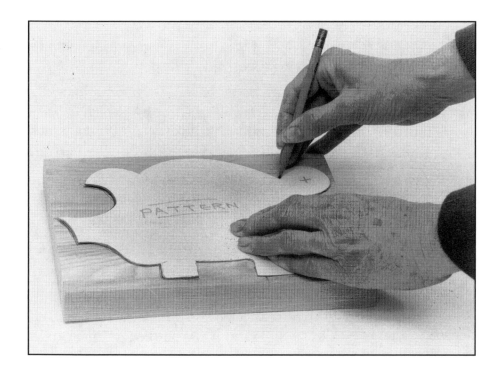

carbon paper (refer to No. 7347 when ordering). This does, however, tend to leave smudges on the wood that can be difficult to remove.

If you intend to make several pieces from one pattern, transfer the pattern to a sheet of heavy cardboard or ⅛-inch plywood and cut it out. You can trace around this template as often as necessary. If the pattern is the exact size and shape on both sides of a line that bisects it, make only half a pattern and trace it once on each side of a line you draw on the wood. This will ensure perfect symmetry.

Finishing

Most of the projects are painted; a few are stained. If you plan to paint, always prime the wood first. I usually use an artist acrylic paint or quick-drying craft enamel in brass (for gold color), chrome (for silver), and bronze. On stained projects, I used walnut. On the one large project, the sled, I used a latex gloss enamel for the green and white areas and artist acrylic for the red pinstripe. These paints dry very quickly, so you can move along much faster with the second coat or detailing.

Sand lightly with very fine No. 220 sandpaper or No. 0000 steel wool between coats. If any project is to be given to a child, you must use non-toxic paint.

For intricate work, stencil or paint by hand. For very fine details, use an ink pen, a very fine liner brush, or woodburning tool. You may prefer a clear natural finish on some projects. For a finishing coat, I use an artist water-based clear satin varnish. Apply two or three coats, sanding lightly between each.

An antique finish gives a project "character." Paint as usual, then sand it in spots where it would have worn through the years. Apply walnut stain or brown shoe polish to all surfaces and quickly wipe it off, especially the walnut stain. The stain will stay in the abraded areas, giving your project an aged look. Finish with a couple of layers of clear satin varnish.

Paste wax gives a satin look and feel. I didn't feel it was necessary on the smaller projects, but used it on the larger ones.

Again, finish your projects as you wish. Experimenting with techniques is part of the fun!

The Projects

Happy New Year

Here is a sign to ring in the new year that can be enlarged to most any size. It could grace a windowsill, a table with a poinsettia, or the buffet for your New Year's Eve party.

MATERIALS:
Clear pine or plywood (thickness depends on size of sign), spray paint. Colors optional.

TOOLS:
Saber or scroll saw, sandpaper.

METHOD:
1. Transfer pattern to wood.
2. Using saber or scroll saw, cut out letters, including interior parts.
3. Sand front and back surfaces.
4. To finish as illustrated, spray all surfaces with a light primer coat. When dry, sand lightly.
5. Spray all surfaces with a coat of black paint.
6. When dry, spray front surface with bronze enamel.
7. Optional: For a gold leaf effect, hand paint a mixed-luster gold enamel over the bronze enamel.
8. Add top coat of clear satin acrylic varnish.

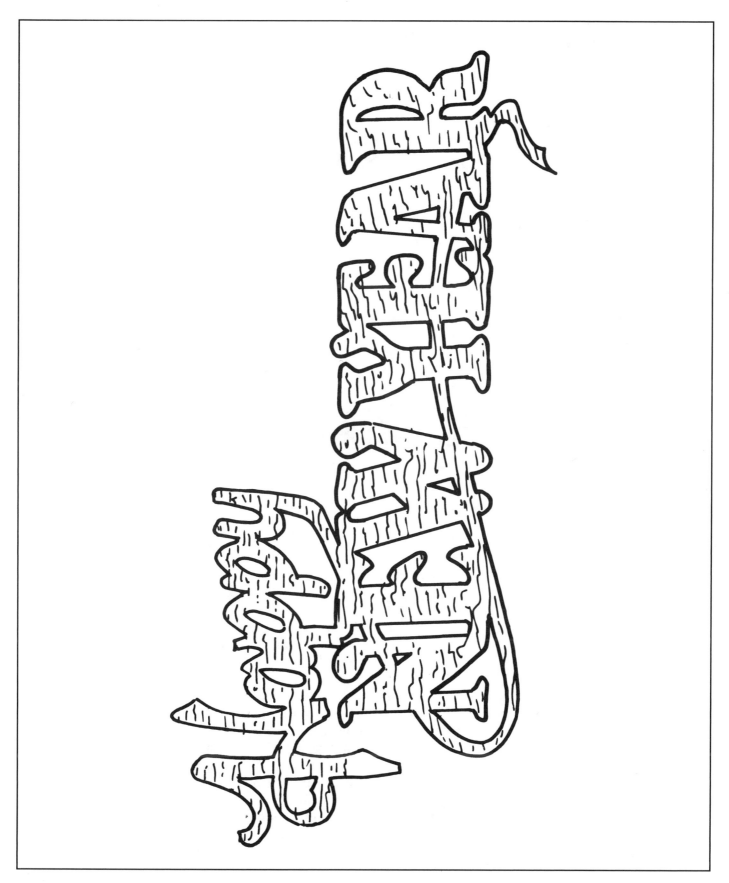

Sponge-Painted Heart Garland

This project enlivens a door or wall. It is quick to make and will be appreciated as a gift.

MATERIALS:

$1/8$-inch to $1/4$-inch plywood, string or twine, sponge, artist acrylic paints, Liquitex acrylic gloss varnish.

TOOLS:

Scroll or band saw, drill, sandpaper.

METHOD:

1. Cut 8 or so $2 1/8$-by-$2 1/2$-inch rectangles out of plywood.
2. Place in a neat pile and tape all together.
3. On the top piece, lay out heart shape and locate the two $1/16$-inch holes.
4. Drill holes through all 8 pieces.
5. Cut out heart shape with all pieces still taped together.
6. Sand edges if needed.
7. Apply ivory paint to all surfaces of each heart.
8. When dry, take a piece of a kitchen sponge and dab a small amount of red iron oxide paint onto front surface of hearts. When dry, paint backs and sides similarly.
9. When dry, apply a finish of high-gloss varnish.
10. Let dry, then redrill holes if necessary and add string.
11. To keep hearts spaced evenly along string, apply a spot of glue on back of each hole.

12

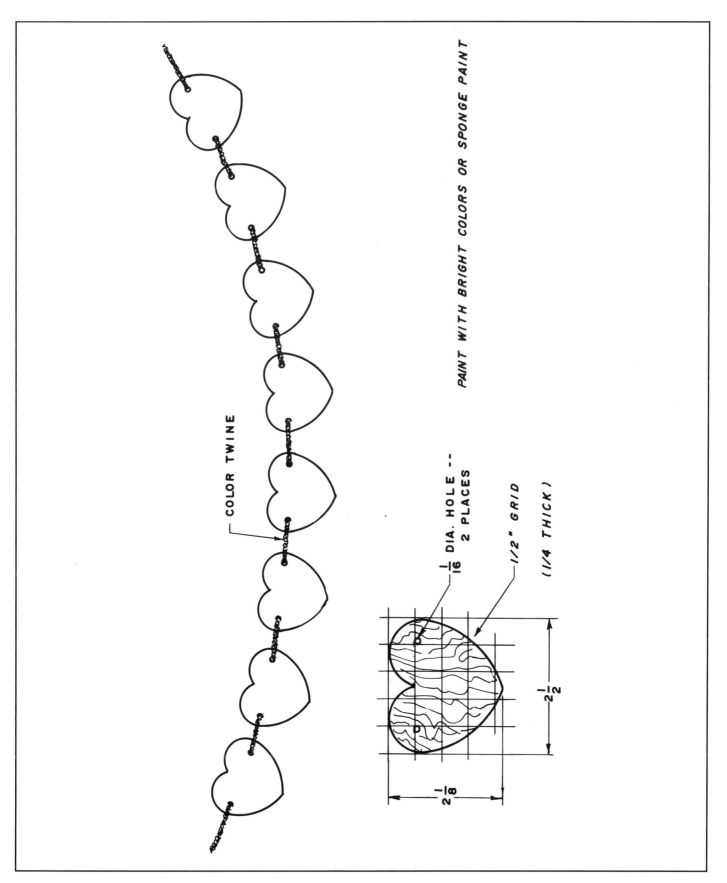

COLOR TWINE

PAINT WITH BRIGHT COLORS OR SPONGE PAINT

$\frac{1}{16}$ DIA. HOLE --
2 PLACES

1/2" GRID

(1/4 THICK)

$2\frac{1}{2}$

$2\frac{1}{8}$

13

Tulip and Heart Wreath

This will bring a bright, happy spring look into your home.

MATERIALS:
3/16-inch to 1/4-inch plywood, 1/8-inch plywood, sawtooth hanger, artist acrylic paint, sponge, walnut stain, clear satin varnish, glue.

TOOLS:
Saber or scroll saw, drill, sandpaper, hammer, compass.

METHOD:
1. Cut 1/8-inch plywood into 8 pieces 2 1/8 by 2 1/2 inches each.
2. Make 2 stacks of 4 pieces each and tape them together.
3. On top piece of each stack, draw pattern as given—heart on one, tulip on the other.
4. Cut out hearts and tulips.
5. Sand all edges.
6. With compass, lay out base directly on a piece of 3/16-inch or 1/4-inch plywood. Locate the eight 3/4-inch holes.
7. Cut out base and drill holes. Sand all edges and surfaces.
8. Prime and paint base an antique white.
9. When dry, apply a light coat of walnut stain. This gives an antique look.
10. Prime tulips and hearts. When dry, paint tulips yellow and hearts red.
11. Optional: Sponge paint tulips a slightly lighter yellow and hearts pink.
12. When dry, apply light coat of walnut stain. Let dry.
13. Locate and glue hearts and tulips around base. Space and locate as shown, centered between holes.
14. Apply top coat of high-gloss varnish.
15. Affix sawtooth hanger (or hanger to suit) on back.

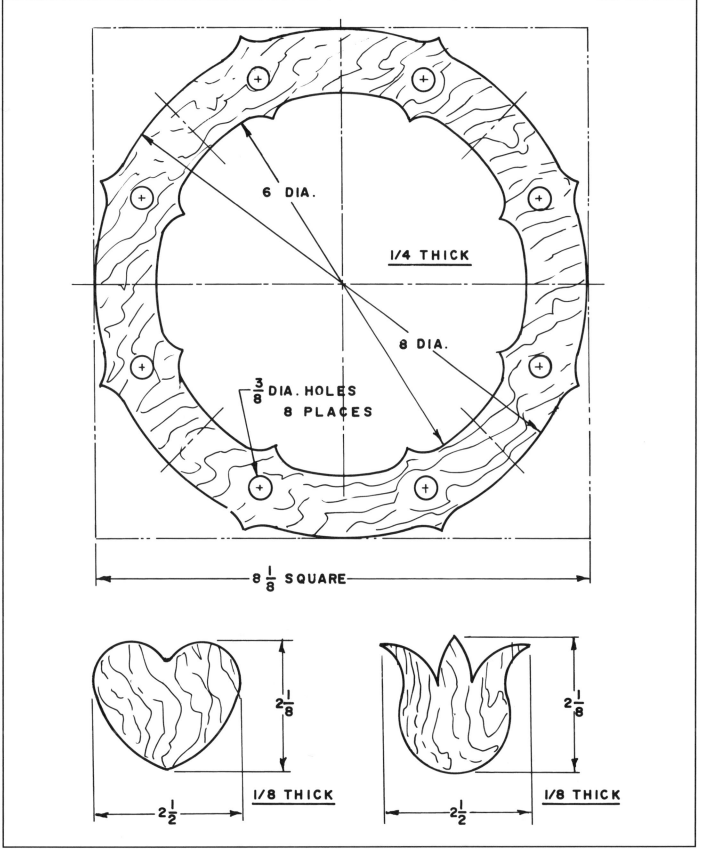

6 DIA.

1/4 THICK

8 DIA.

$\frac{3}{8}$ DIA. HOLES
8 PLACES

$8\frac{1}{8}$ SQUARE

$2\frac{1}{8}$

1/8 THICK

$2\frac{1}{2}$

$2\frac{1}{8}$

1/8 THICK

$2\frac{1}{2}$

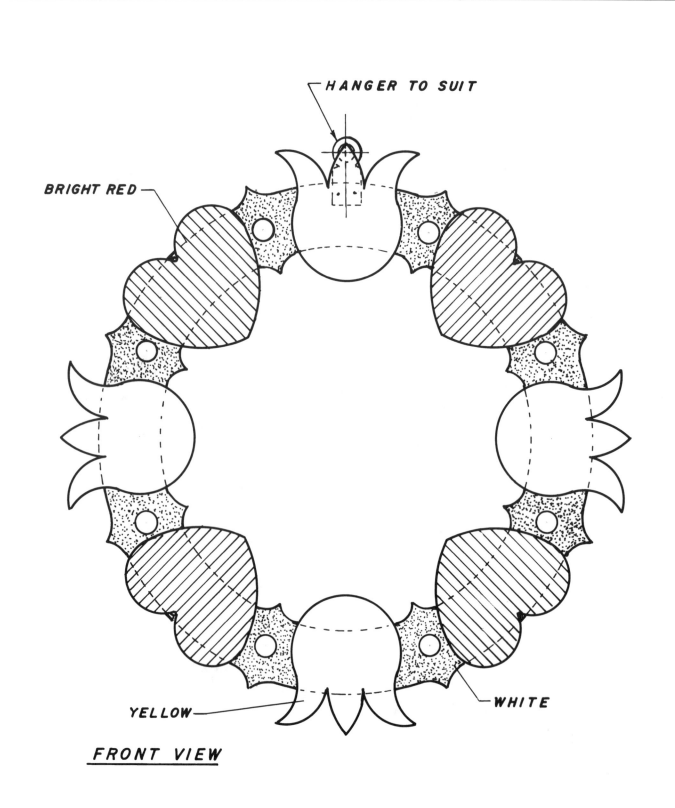

HANGER TO SUIT

BRIGHT RED

YELLOW

WHITE

FRONT VIEW

16

George and Martha Washington Profiles

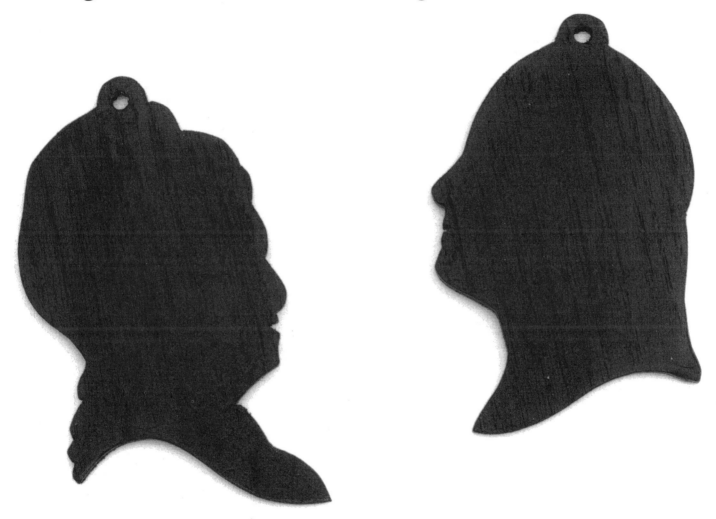

This makes a memorable display around Presidents Day in February, but could be used anytime as a Colonial decoration.

MATERIALS:
1/8-inch to 1/4-inch plywood, black paint, sandpaper, sawtooth hangers, varnish.

TOOLS:
Scroll saw, drill.

METHOD:
1. Transfer pattern to wood.
2. Cut out heads.
3. Sand all surfaces.
4. Cover all surfaces with black artist acrylic paint.
5. Apply top coat of clear satin varnish.

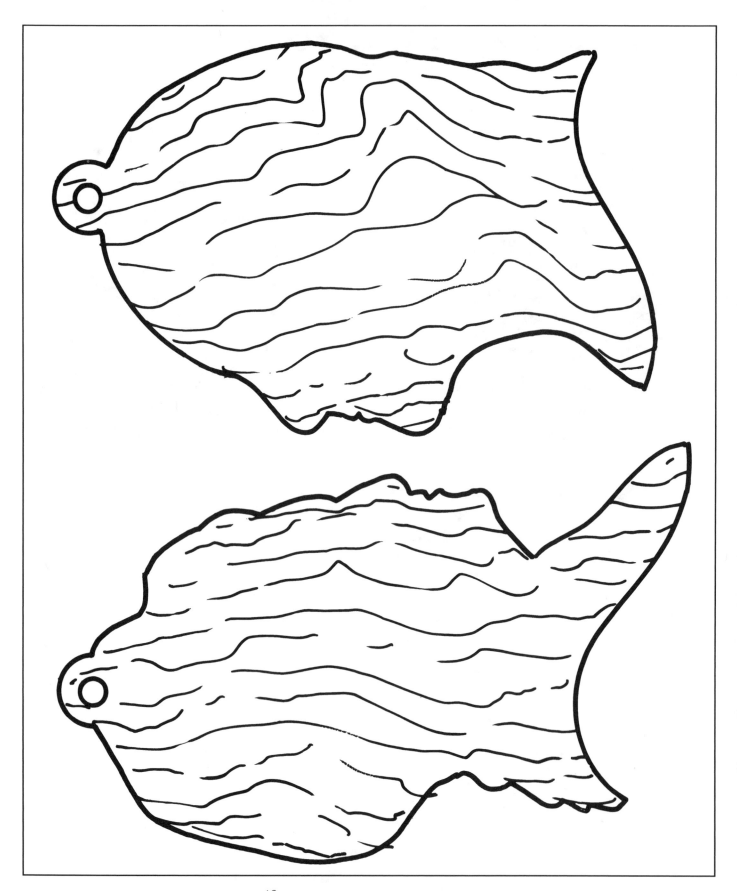

Easter Ornament (Rabbits and Cottage)

Rabbit decorations in all sizes and shapes are always popular around Easter. This project will make good use of your scroll saw skills.

MATERIALS:

1/8-inch plywood, sandpaper, artist acrylic paint, varnish.

TOOLS:

Scroll saw, drill.

METHOD:

1. Transfer pattern to wood.
2. Carefully cut out. With difficult patterns such as this, try making a copy and affixing it to wood with rubber cement. Remove copy after cutting out project.
3. Paint lower area (the "grass") with a coat of green paint thinned with water. Use a dabbing motion.
4. Use same green with a touch of brown to make tree leaves. Again, use dabbing motion.
5. Paint tree burnt umber.
6. Paint rabbits antique white with pink on ears, tip of nose, tail. Use dabbing motion again.
7. Paint eyes black with wooden end of brush.
8. Paint cottage antique white, with golden brown for shading and roof.
9. Paint chimney, window edges, loop at top of ornament pink.
10. Finish with high-gloss varnish.

Egg with 3 Rabbits

At Eastertime, anything can happen; a rabbit can even hatch from an egg! This was originally used in the 1920s. You'll love it.

MATERIALS:

1/2-inch to 3/4-inch pine, sandpaper, primer, artist acrylic paint, varnish, brown shoe polish.

TOOLS:

Saber or scroll saw.

METHOD:

1. Transfer pattern to wood.
2. Cut out and sand all edges.
3. Prime. When dry, paint egg a light ivory. Rabbits are ivory plus a dab of golden brown on your brush. A light dabbing or bouncing motion creates look of fur. Use burnt umber and light ivory for shading and highlighting.
4. Add burnt umber for eyes, nose, whiskers.
5. When egg is dry, wipe on brown shoe polish for shading. Along edges, this gives illusion of egg being round.
6. Apply a top coat of clear satin varnish.

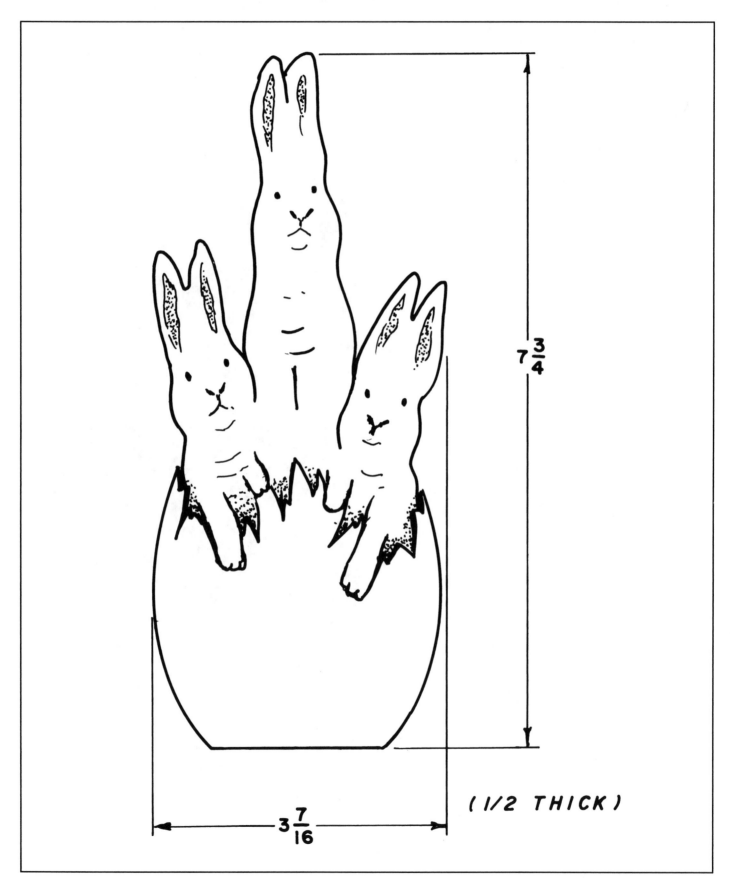

$7\dfrac{3}{4}$

$(1/2\ THICK)$

$3\dfrac{7}{16}$

Chick Pulling Cart

Chicks are another symbol of the renewal of life in the springtime. This project is a copy of an ornament from the early 1900s. To antique it, I used a folk art technique that leaves a crackled finish.

MATERIALS:

$1/2$-inch and $3/4$-inch pine, two $2^1/2$-inch diameter pewter wheels, 2 tacks for axle, 3 brads, ribbon or yarn, scraps of pine, sandpaper, primer, paint, folk art crackle (optional), sponge, walnut stain, satin acrylic varnish.

TOOLS:

Scroll saw, table saw, hammer, small drill.

METHOD:

1. Transfer pattern of chick to $1/2$-inch-thick piece of pine.
2. Transfer pattern of egg to $3/4$-inch-thick piece of pine.
3. Cut both patterns out and sand all edges lightly. Note egg is flat along bottom edge.
4. For base of wagon, cut a $1/4$-inch-thick piece of wood $1^3/8$ by 4 inches.
5. Cut two $8^1/8$-inch-long shafts from scraps that are $1/4$ inch square.
6. Glue the shafts to the base about $5/8$ inch apart, as shown.
7. Cut a $1^3/8$-inch-long piece for the axle $3/8$ by $1/2$ inch. Glue this piece to bottom of axle about $1^1/2$ inches in from back of base of wagon.
8. Prime chick and egg.
9. Paint wagon assembly with burnt umber and add wheels. This completes wagon.
10. Paint chick and egg antique white.
11. Paint chick light yellow, using a sponge. A swirling motion gives effect of feathers.

12. Paint the chick's comb adobe. A mixture of adobe and antique gold is used for beak, legs, feet. Paint collar on chick a dusty mauve. If eye is drilled out on chick, use black for inside of hole.
13. When chick is dry, apply folk art crackle medium. Let this dry up to 4 hours, then apply coat of light yellow paint, making sure not to overlap strokes. After this dries, you should have the crackle finish and aged look.
14. Finish by rubbing all surfaces of chick with walnut stain. When dry, apply clear satin varnish.
15. Transfer pattern to painted egg.
16. Paint pattern on egg, using dusty mauve, rose, pink, yellow, liberty blue, Christmas green, deep river green.
17. When dry, attach chick to cart with 2 small brads. Add a brad to front of cart to hold yarn or ribbon.
18. Glue egg in place and add ribbon (refer to drawing).

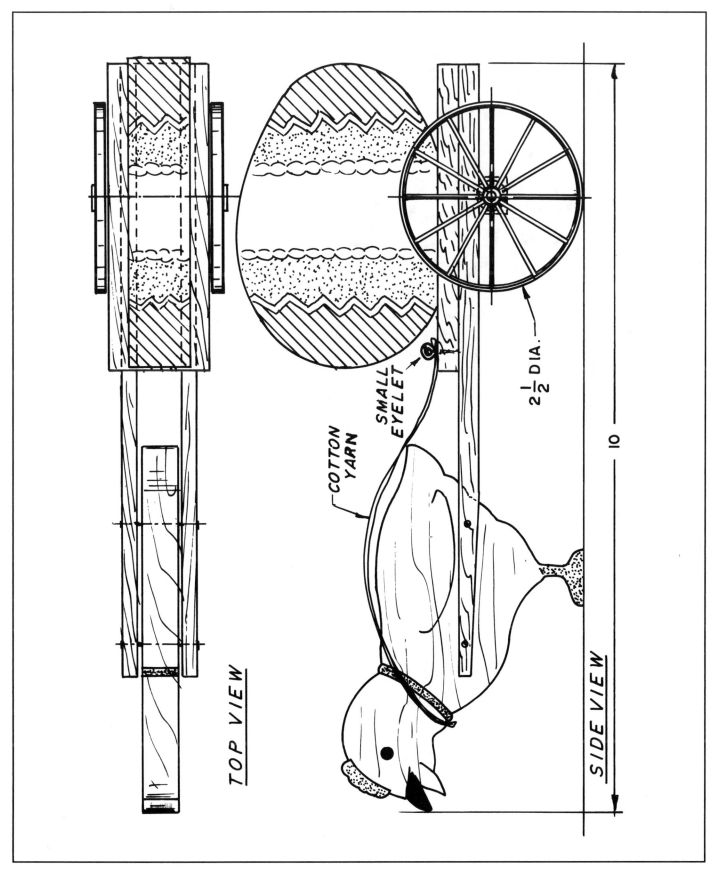

TOP VIEW

COTTON YARN

SMALL EYELET

$2\frac{1}{2}$ DIA.

10

SIDE VIEW

25

Rabbit on Wheels

This is a copy of an old pull toy. I especially like it because it can be used all year long to spruce up a windowsill, bookcase, or planter.

MATERIALS:
1/4-inch and 3/4-inch pine, sandpaper, artist acrylic paint, folk art crackle medium, varnish, 1/4-inch dowel, 1 1/4-inch dowel.

TOOLS:
Band or scroll saw, hammer, drill.

METHOD:
1. On a 3/4-inch piece of pine, transfer pattern of body and wheels. Locate all holes.
2. On a 1/4-inch piece of pine, transfer pattern of front and back legs. Locate all holes.
3. Cut out body, legs, wheels. Sand all surfaces lightly. Sand front wheel so it is 11/16 inch thick.
4. Drill all 1/4-inch holes in all pieces, including back wheels, as shown.
5. Cut all dowels to length. Note 2 back wheels are cut 1/2 inch thick from a 1 1/4-inch dowel.
6. Glue legs to body, making sure they align as shown.
7. Paint all pieces with pink artist acrylic.
8. Optional: When dry, apply a crackle medium. For small cracks, apply a thin coat; for large cracks, apply a heavy coat. Allow to dry up to 4 hours.
9. When dry, apply mauve paint to all pieces. When applying this, do not overlap strokes or restroke. Let dry. This coat gives the cracks, or old look.
10. Add a top coat of walnut stain. When dry, apply satin varnish.
11. Redrill all 1/4-inch holes and assemble wheels and axles. Glue in place.
12. Everything should turn correctly. Adjust if necessary.

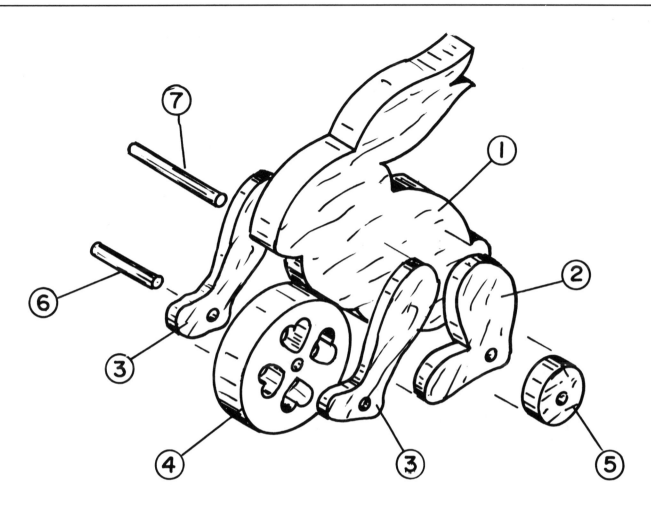

EXPLODED VIEW

NO.	NAME	SIZE	REQ'D.
1	BODY	3/4 X 6 5/8 – 6 7/8	1
2	BACK LEG	1/4 X 2 1/4 – 3 1/8 LG.	2
3	FRONT LEG	1/4 X 1 1/4 – 3 3/4	2
4	FRONT WHEEL	11/16 X 2 1/2 DIA.	1
5	BACK WHEEL	1/2 X 1 1/4 DIA.	2
6	FRONT AXLE	1/4 DIA. X 1 3/8 LG.	1
7	BACK AXLE	1/4 DIA. X 2 3/8 LG.	1

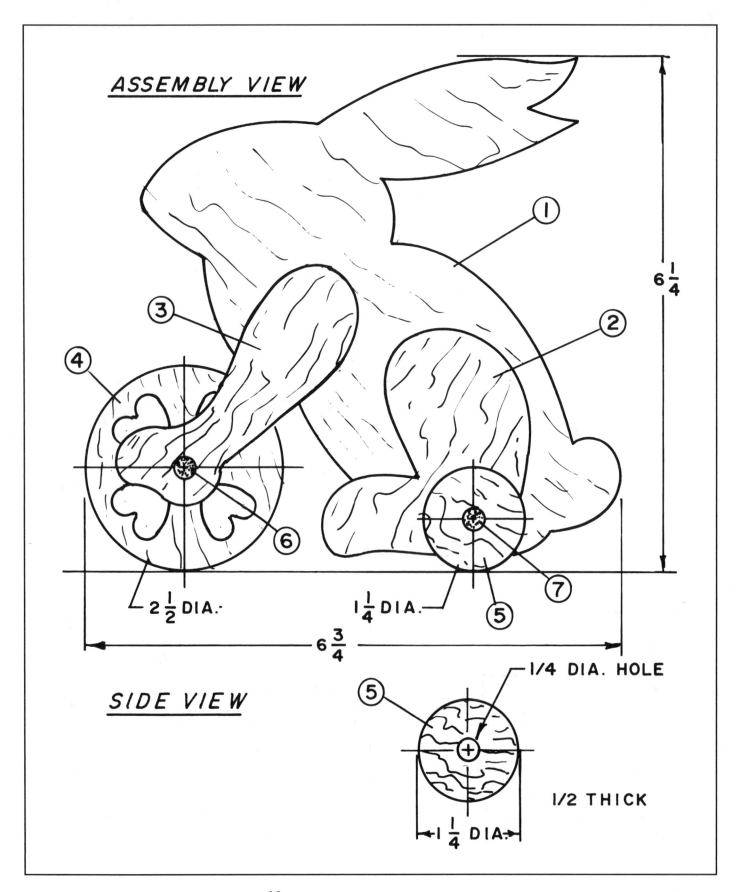

ASSEMBLY VIEW

①

③

④

②

$6\frac{1}{4}$

⑥

$2\frac{1}{2}$ DIA.

$1\frac{1}{4}$ DIA.

⑤

⑦

$6\frac{3}{4}$

SIDE VIEW

⑤ 1/4 DIA. HOLE

1/2 THICK

$1\frac{1}{4}$ DIA.

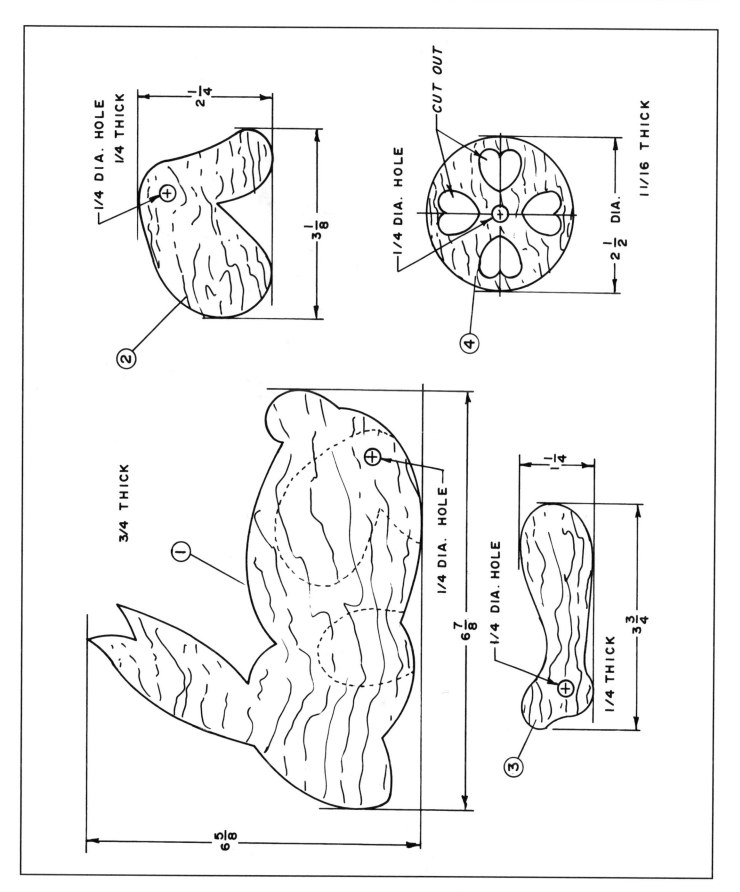

1/4 DIA. HOLE
1/4 THICK

$2\frac{1}{4}$

$3\frac{1}{8}$

②

CUT OUT

1/4 DIA. HOLE

$2\frac{1}{2}$ DIA.

11/16 THICK

④

3/4 THICK

①

1/4 DIA. HOLE

$6\frac{7}{8}$

$6\frac{5}{8}$

$1\frac{1}{4}$

1/4 DIA. HOLE

1/4 THICK

$3\frac{3}{4}$

③

29

Rabbit Basket Holder

No one will forget an Easter basket full of candy and eggs when it's presented in a stand held by four bunnies.

MATERIALS:
5-by-28-inch piece of ½-inch pine, sandpaper, artist acrylic paint, walnut stain, satin varnish.

TOOLS:
Band or scroll saw.

METHOD:
1. Lay out full-size pattern using 1-inch grid (left side). Include ½-inch slot in middle.
2. Transfer pattern to wood.
3. Cut out pattern. Slot in center must be cut from top (as shown) in one piece and bottom in other.
4. Glue pieces together at right angles.
5. Prime. When dry, paint an off-white color.
6. Paint whiskers black with a thin liner brush.
7. Paint grass area green.
8. Apply walnut stain for an antique look.
9. Paint eyes or, if you prefer, add ½-inch-size jiggly eyes.

Note: Distance between rabbits may be adjusted for a particular basket.

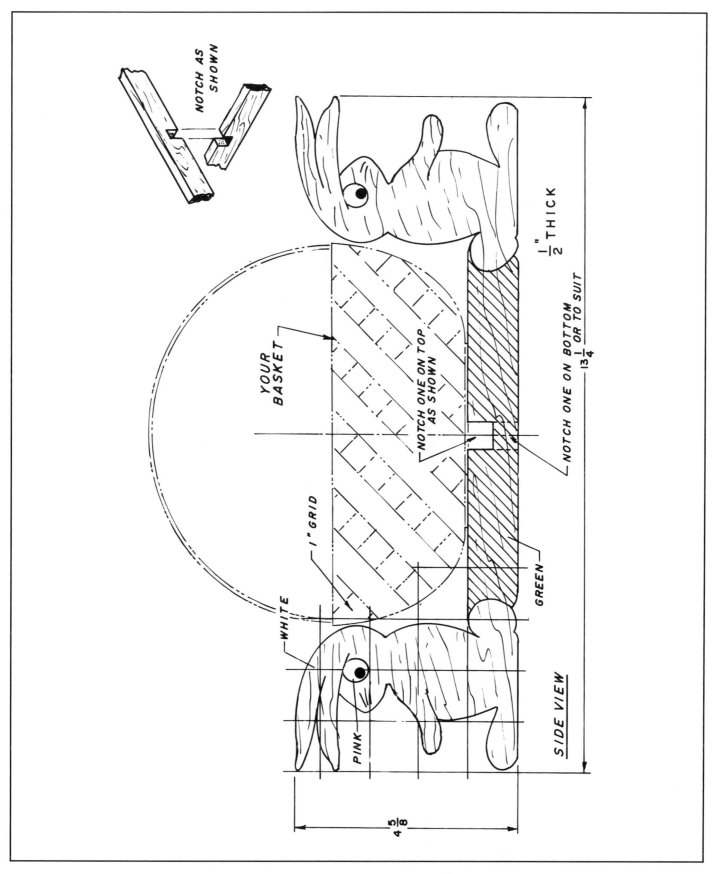

NOTCH AS SHOWN

$\frac{1}{2}$" THICK

NOTCH ONE ON BOTTOM
$13\frac{1}{4}$ OR TO SUIT

NOTCH ONE ON TOP
AS SHOWN

YOUR BASKET

1" GRID

WHITE

PINK

GREEN

$4\frac{5}{8}$

SIDE VIEW

31

Rabbit on a Stick

This simple spring project will make winter disappear. It can be the focus of a spring flower display or an Easter mantle decoration. It also can be a year-round decoration.

MATERIALS:

3/4-inch pine, 3/8-inch dowel (10 inches long), 1-inch sphere, sandpaper, artist acrylic paint, sponge, satin varnish.

TOOLS:

Band or scroll saw, drill, router (optional).

METHOD:

1. Lay out full-size pattern using 1-inch grid.
2. Transfer pattern to wood.
3. Cut out all parts, including oval base. Make a matched pair of front and back legs.
4. Drill a 3/8-inch hole through body and base, as shown.
5. Optional: Using a router with a 1/8-inch cove cutter, make cove cut around base.
6. Glue legs to body as shown.
7. Attach rabbit and sphere to dowel and glue all into base.
8. Prime all surfaces. When dry, paint rabbit Navajo white.
9. When dry, sponge paint golden brown spots all over rabbit.
10. Paint stand and sphere golden brown.
11. Finish with coat of clear satin varnish.

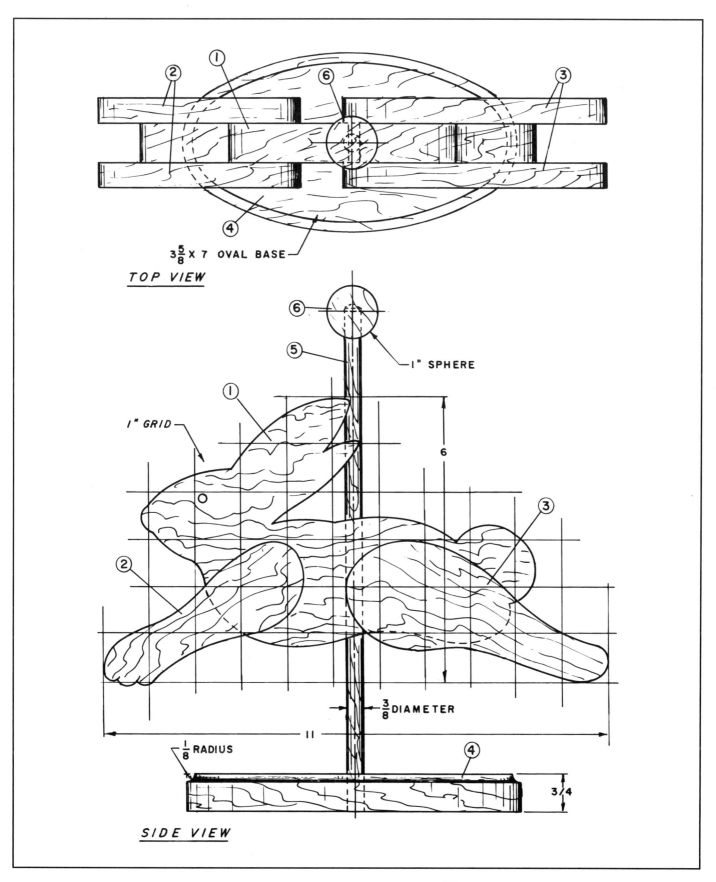

③ ② ① ⑥ ③

④

$3\frac{5}{8}$ X 7 OVAL BASE

TOP VIEW

⑥

⑤

1" SPHERE

① 1" GRID

③

② O

6

$\frac{3}{8}$ DIAMETER

11

$\frac{1}{8}$ RADIUS

④

3/4

SIDE VIEW

Rabbit Pulling Wagon

This festive project, also based on an antique, will really get the Easter season rolling. The wagon can be filled with Easter candy or an egg.

MATERIALS:
3/16-inch-diameter dowels, 3/8-inch-diameter dowels, 1/2-inch-diameter dowels, 1/4-inch-thick pine scraps, brads, sandpaper, artist acrylic paint, walnut stain, glue.

TOOLS:
Scroll saw, drill, No. 8 round paint brush.

METHOD:
1. Transfer patterns to wood.
2. Cut out pieces. Drill all holes and sand all surfaces.
3. Make all pieces for wagon as shown. Assemble, but don't add wheels.
4. Attach center pull shaft.
5. Assemble rabbit with 3/8-inch spacers.
6. Prime all parts.
7. Paint rabbit and small wheels antique white. When dry, wipe all surfaces with walnut stain for antique look.
8. Wagon is painted dusty mauve; undercarriage, liberty blue. Paint rear wheels yellow with liberty blue rims.
9. Optional: Add pattern to rear wheels with a variety of bright colors. Use No. 8 round brush for comma designs and half-circles. Use wooden end of brush for dots.
10. Apply top coat of clear satin varnish.
11. Assemble wheels. They should turn freely.
12. Add Easter candy or egg to wagon.

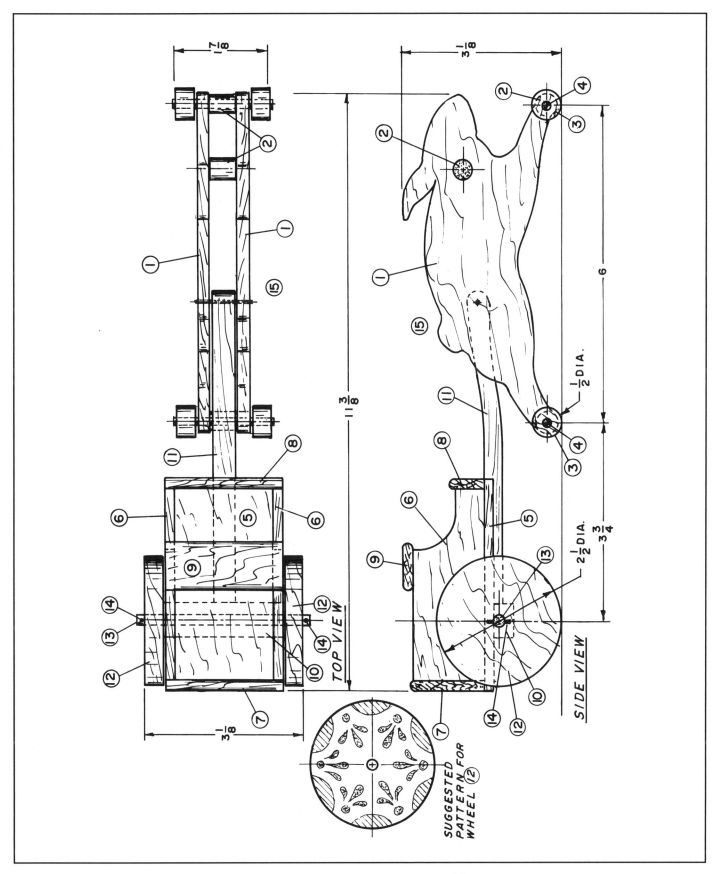

$\frac{7}{8}$

$3\frac{1}{8}$

② ④

② ③

②

①

$\frac{1}{2}$ DIA.

6

④

③

⑮

①

①

⑮

⑪

⑪

⑧

⑧

⑥

⑥

⑤

⑨

② ⑤

$2\frac{1}{2}$ DIA.

$3\frac{3}{4}$

⑥

⑨

⑬

④ ⑨

⑭

⑩

⑫

⑭ ⑩

⑫

⑭

⑬

⑫

$11\frac{3}{8}$

⑦

TOP VIEW

SIDE VIEW

$3\frac{1}{8}$

⑦

SUGGESTED PATTERN FOR WHEEL ⑫

35

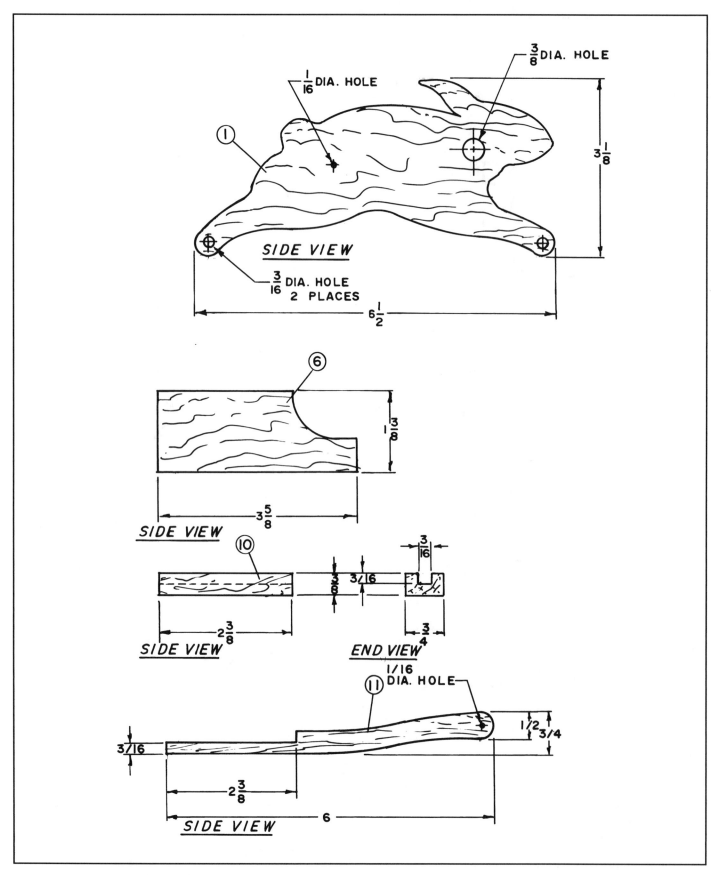

$\frac{1}{16}$DIA. HOLE

$\frac{3}{8}$DIA. HOLE

① SIDE VIEW

$\frac{3}{16}$ DIA. HOLE
2 PLACES

$3\frac{1}{8}$

$6\frac{1}{2}$

⑥

$1\frac{3}{8}$

SIDE VIEW

$3\frac{5}{8}$

⑩

$\frac{3}{8}$ 3/16

$\frac{3}{16}$

SIDE VIEW

$2\frac{3}{8}$

END VIEW

$\frac{3}{4}$

1/16
DIA. HOLE

⑪

1/2 3/4

3/16

$2\frac{3}{8}$

6

SIDE VIEW

36

Sandpiper on a Stick

These simple-to-make decoys are stunning summer decorations, especially for the beach house. Add a red ribbon to the neck and you could even use it at Christmastime.

MATERIALS:
Pine scraps, dowel, artist acrylic paint, walnut stain, paste wax, varnish.

TOOLS:
Scroll saw, drill, sandpaper.

METHOD:
1. Transfer pattern to wood so that tail runs parallel to grain.
2. Cut out bird and sand all surfaces.
3. Prime. When dry, paint body with a wash coat (gray and white paint mixed and watered down).
4. Drill out eye hole.
5. Paint beak and leg yellow or black.
6. Apply walnut stain to base (stand).
7. When dry, add a top coat of satin varnish. Let dry and apply paste wax to all surfaces.

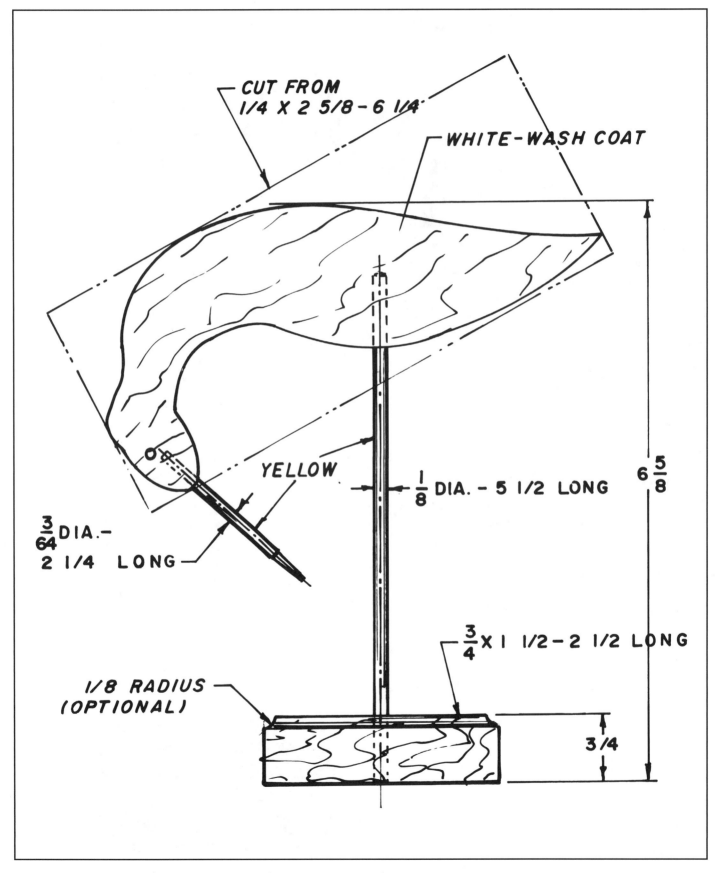

CUT FROM
1/4 X 2 5/8 - 6 1/4

WHITE-WASH COAT

YELLOW

$\frac{1}{8}$ DIA. - 5 1/2 LONG

$6\frac{5}{8}$

$\frac{3}{64}$ DIA. -
2 1/4 LONG

$\frac{3}{4}$ X 1 1/2 - 2 1/2 LONG

1/8 RADIUS
(OPTIONAL)

3/4

Girl with Watering Can

If you love to place flowers and plants all over the house, this project will add a special touch to your pots and planters. The pattern was found in an antique shop. You may use it in the garden after applying a coat of polyurethane varnish.

MATERIALS:
¹/₄-inch-thick scrap wood, artist acrylic paint, clear satin varnish or polyurethane.

TOOLS:
Scroll or band saw.

METHOD:
1. Transfer pattern to wood.
2. Cut out. You may make 3 or 4 at a time by stacking pieces of wood.
3. Prime. When dry, sand lightly.
4. Paint hat, dress, socks red. Rims of hat and shoe are white; watering can is yellow.
5. When dry, add a top coat of clear satin varnish or, for outdoor use, apply a top coat of polyurethane varnish instead.

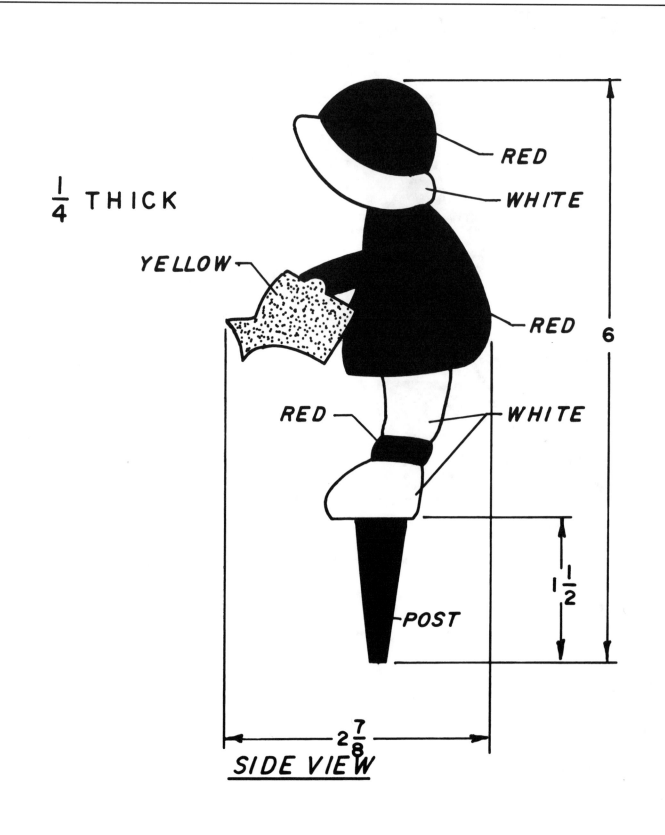

$\frac{1}{4}$ THICK

YELLOW

RED

WHITE

RED

6

RED

WHITE

POST

$1\frac{1}{2}$

$2\frac{7}{8}$

SIDE VIEW

Rabbit

Here is another spring decoration that can double as a cutting board. Whether you display it as a cutting board or a decoration, you'll get lots of compliments.

MATERIALS:
¾-inch hardwood (such as maple or cherry), sandpaper, artist acrylic paint, stain, sponge, paintbrush, vegetable oil.

METHOD:
1. Transfer pattern to wood.
2. Carefully cut out and sand all edges slightly.
3. Apply light walnut stain to both sides.
4. If this is a cutting board, rub in a coat or two of vegetable oil on one side. Do not get oil on edges or other side.
5. On the other side, sponge paint body and head with ivory. This gives the effect of fur; color of wood will show through sponge strokes and give it shading.
6. Lightly sponge paint 2 or 3 black spots over ivory. Make sure they are light. Before painting, dab excess paint from sponge onto piece of paper or palette.
7. Outline eye with liner brush and black paint. Inside of eye is pink with a dot of black in center.
8. When dry, apply clear satin varnish on painted side and edges only.

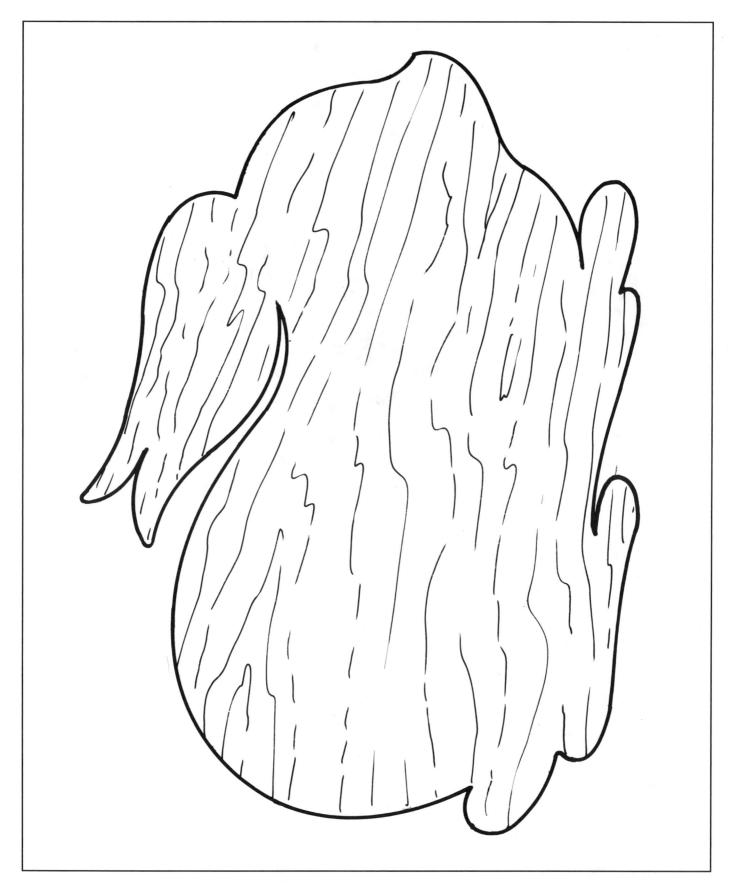

Tulips in Pot

These are simple to make and add a bright, colorful focus to any room.

MATERIALS:
1/2-inch to 3/4-inch scrap wood, sandpaper, No. 10 round brush, varnish.

TOOLS:
Band or scroll saw.

METHOD:
1. Transfer pattern to wood.
2. Cut out. You may stack 2 or 3 and cut out together. Sand all surfaces lightly.
3. Prime. When dry, sand lightly.
4. For clay pot color, mix a little brown into red paint. Mix the paint only lightly and it will give a nice shading effect.
5. Paint stems and leaves a deep river green.
6. Paint smaller tulips antique white adobe, larger tulips white and sunbright yellow. Use a No. 10 round brush. Pull brush through one color, then pull through other color. Long, sweeping strokes give a nice shaded effect.
7. When dry, apply a top coat of clear satin varnish.

43

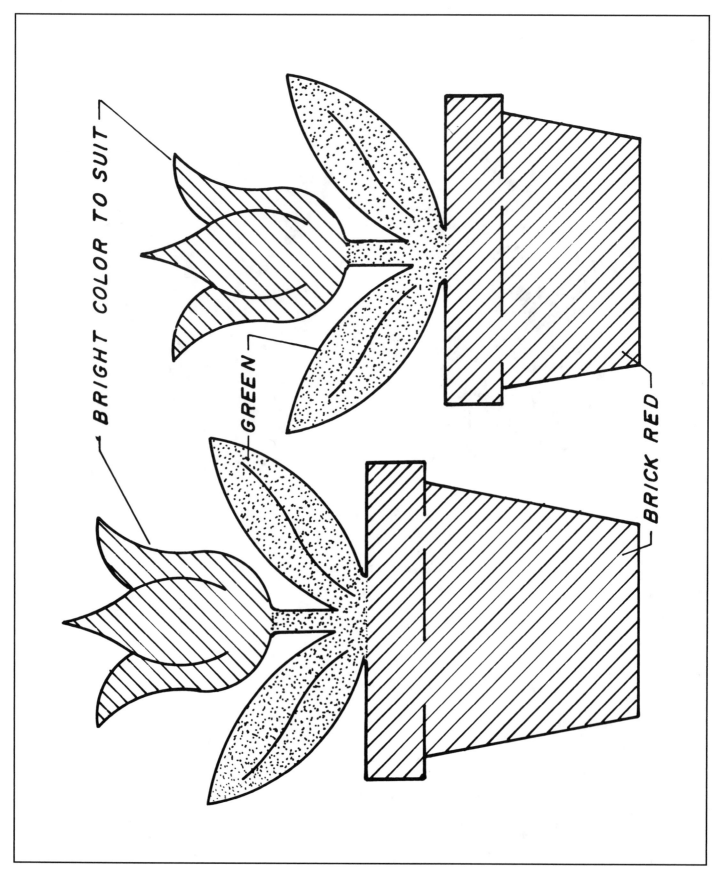

Lamb

This is a wonderful spring decoration that can double as a cutting board.

MATERIALS:

3/4-inch hardwood (such as maple or cherry), sandpaper, artist acrylic paint, stain, sponge, paintbrush, vegetable oil.

TOOLS:

Band or scroll saw.

METHOD:

1. Transfer pattern to wood.
2. Carefully cut out and sand all edges slightly.
3. Apply light walnut stain to both sides.
4. If this is to be a cutting board, rub in a coat or two of vegetable oil on one side. Do not get oil on edges or other side.
5. On the other side, sponge paint body and head with antique white. Sponge paint legs, nose with black.
6. Carefully outline ear with liner brush and black paint.
7. Apply clear satin varnish on dry painted side and edges.

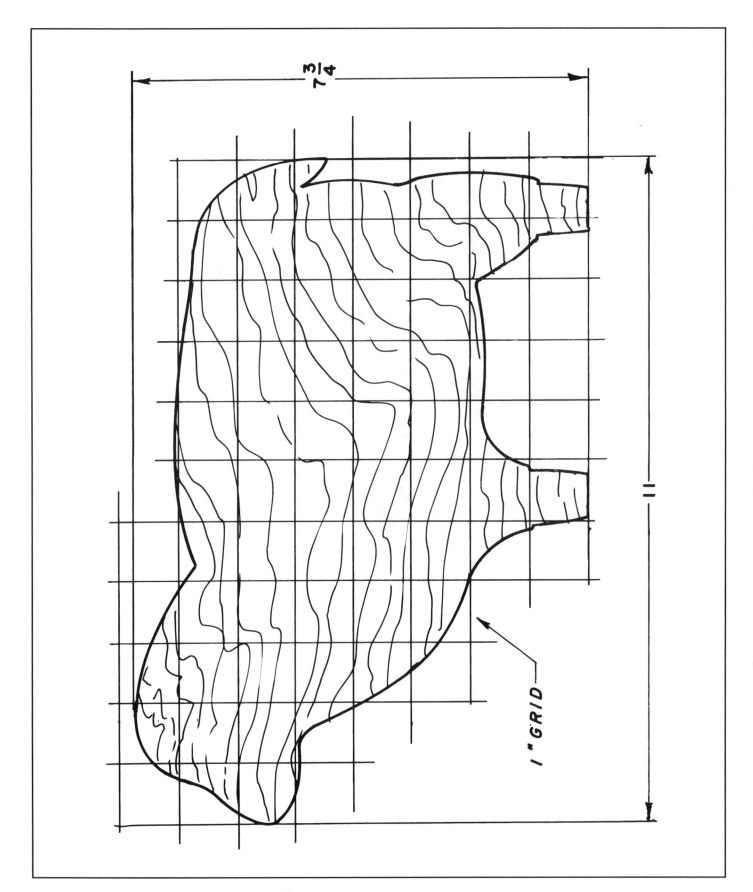

3/4

1"GRID

Small Birdhouse
Long Birdhouse

These are sure signs of spring. If you make several, you can use up a lot of scrap wood while also providing safe nesting space for your decorative wooden birds.

MATERIALS:
Scrap wood, eyelets, dowels, sandpaper, string or twine, paint, satin varnish.

TOOLS:
Saw, drill.

METHOD:
1. Cut scrap wood to the sizes given. Make 8 to 10 at a time. The body of the houses can be made of 2-by-4-inch scraps, or simply glue up two 3/4-inch-thick pieces to come up with 1 1/2-inch material.
2. Drill all holes.
3. Glue roof to house.
4. Prime. When dry, paint with bright colors.
5. Add a top coat of clear satin varnish.
6. Add eyelets for hanging and attach string or twine.

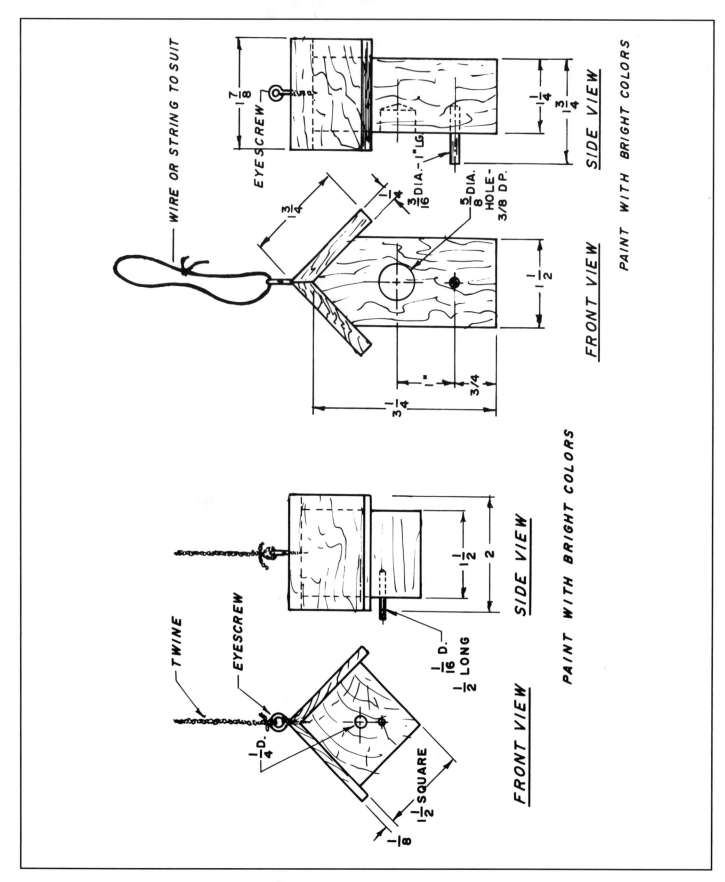

WIRE OR STRING TO SUIT

EYESCREW

SIDE VIEW

FRONT VIEW

PAINT WITH BRIGHT COLORS

$1\frac{7}{8}$

$3\frac{1}{4}$

$1\frac{1}{4}$

$\frac{3}{16}$ DIA.

$\frac{3}{4}$

$1\frac{1}{4}$

$\frac{5}{8}$ DIA. HOLE - 3/8 D.P.

$\frac{3}{16}$ DIA. - 1" LG.

$1\frac{1}{2}$

1"

3/4

$3\frac{1}{4}$

TWINE

EYESCREW

SIDE VIEW

FRONT VIEW

PAINT WITH BRIGHT COLORS

2

$1\frac{1}{2}$

$\frac{1}{16}$ D. $\frac{1}{2}$ LONG

$\frac{1}{4}$ D.

$1\frac{1}{2}$ SQUARE

$\frac{1}{8}$

A Tree
of Birds

Celebrate the return of your neighborhood birds with your own hand-crafted springtime display. A large "tree" will spruce up the dining table or sideboard; a small one will highlight a windowsill or mantle. Patterns are included for several kinds of birds. The blackbird can be painted as a robin or bluebird, and the crested bird can be a blue jay or cardinal. Copy realistic colors and markings from a field guide. If you prefer a folk art look, use less detail and then "distress" the finish by sanding the painted edges and wiping black paint into the nicks and scratches.

MATERIALS:
Scrap wood, artist acrylic paint, tree branch, 3-inch piece of log or block of wood, glue, sandpaper, wire hanger, clear satin varnish.

TOOLS:
Scroll or jig saw, pliers, wood rasp.

METHOD:
1. Transfer pattern to wood so that bird's tail runs parallel to grain.
2. Cut out.
3. Taper body and head into neck with a rasp.
4. Round off edges with sandpaper, as if piece were a well-worn antique.
5. For canary, paint yellow, black, white.
6. For dove, paint gray, white, brown tones.
7. For blue jay, paint blue, black, white, gray.
8. For cardinal, paint red, white, black.
9. For blackbird, paint black, white, red.
10. When dry, apply top coat of varnish.
11. Select a branch sturdy enough to support birds. Cut wire hanger into 2-inch lengths. Insert one end into body of a bird; bend the other so it will fit around a branch.
12. Drill a hole in center of a log or block of wood. End of branch must fit in hole. Add a few drops of glue to hole and insert branch.
13. Perch bird or birds in tree.

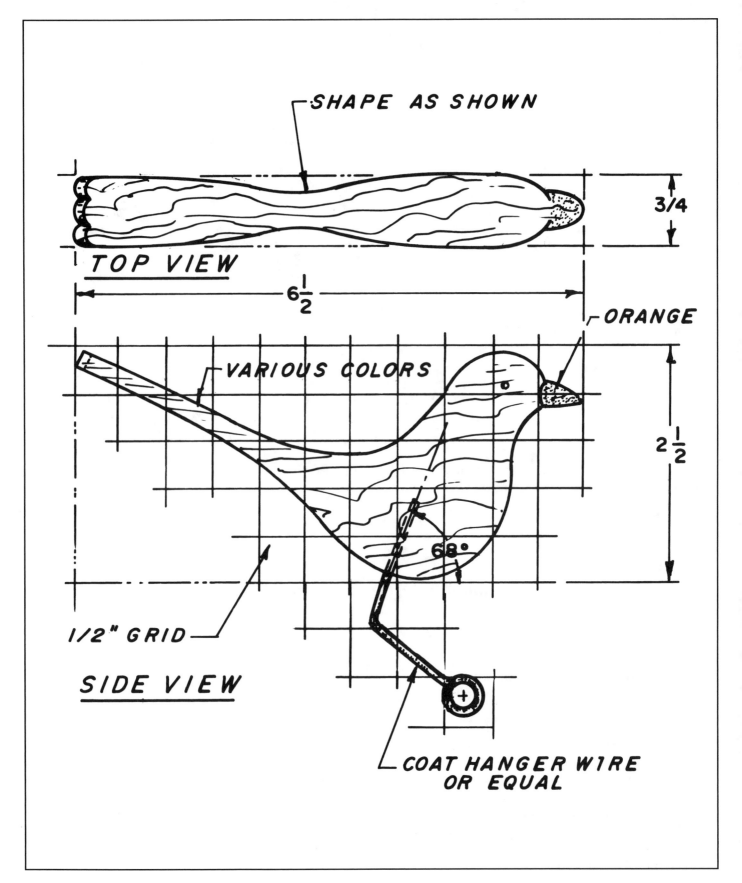

SHAPE AS SHOWN

3/4

TOP VIEW

6½

ORANGE

VARIOUS COLORS

2½

68°

1/2" GRID

SIDE VIEW

COAT HANGER WIRE
OR EQUAL

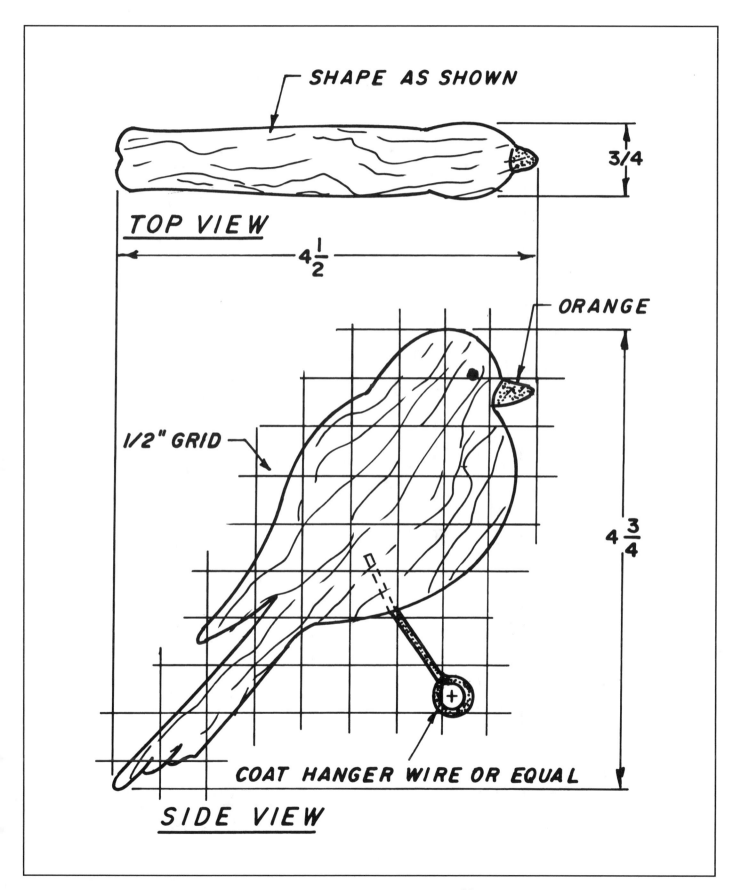

SHAPE AS SHOWN

3/4

TOP VIEW

4 1/2

ORANGE

1/2" GRID

4 3/4

COAT HANGER WIRE OR EQUAL

SIDE VIEW

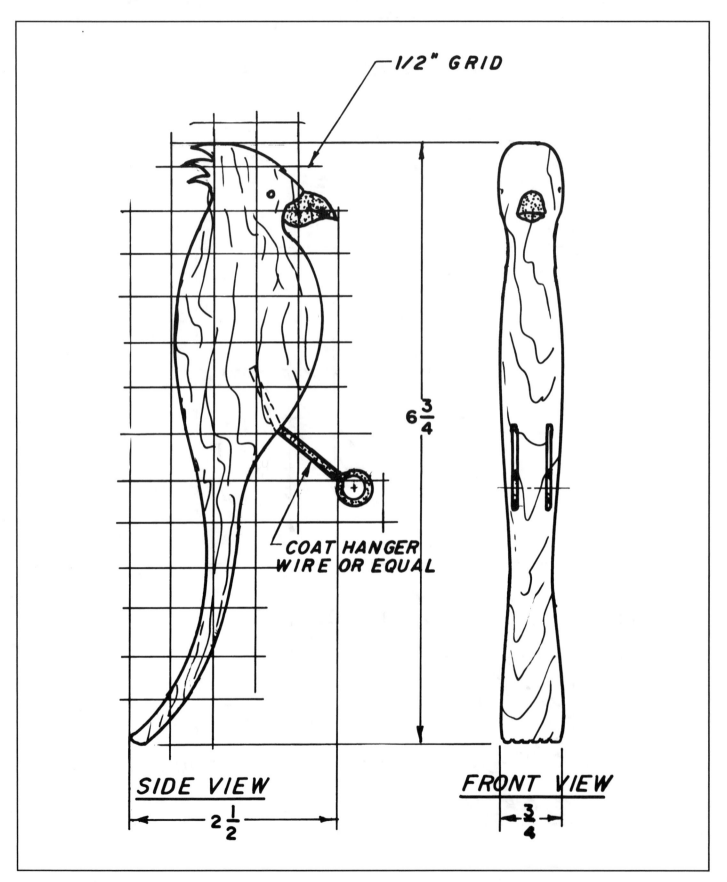

1/2" GRID

6 3/4

COAT HANGER
WIRE OR EQUAL

SIDE VIEW
2 1/2

FRONT VIEW
3/4

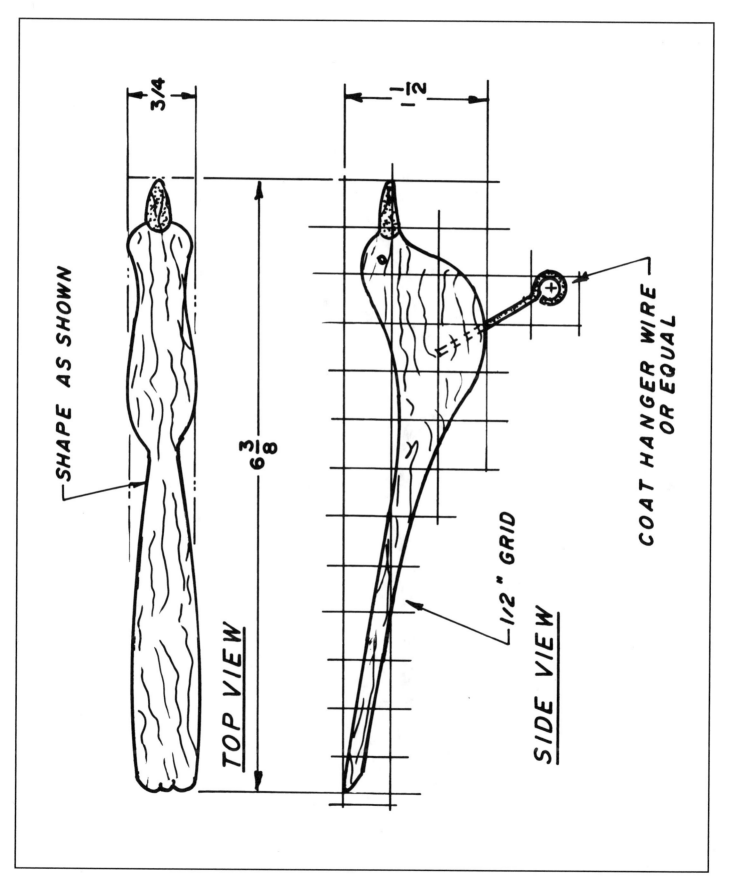

SHAPE AS SHOWN

3/4

$6\frac{3}{8}$

TOP VIEW

$1\frac{1}{2}$

1/2" GRID

SIDE VIEW

COAT HANGER WIRE OR EQUAL

53

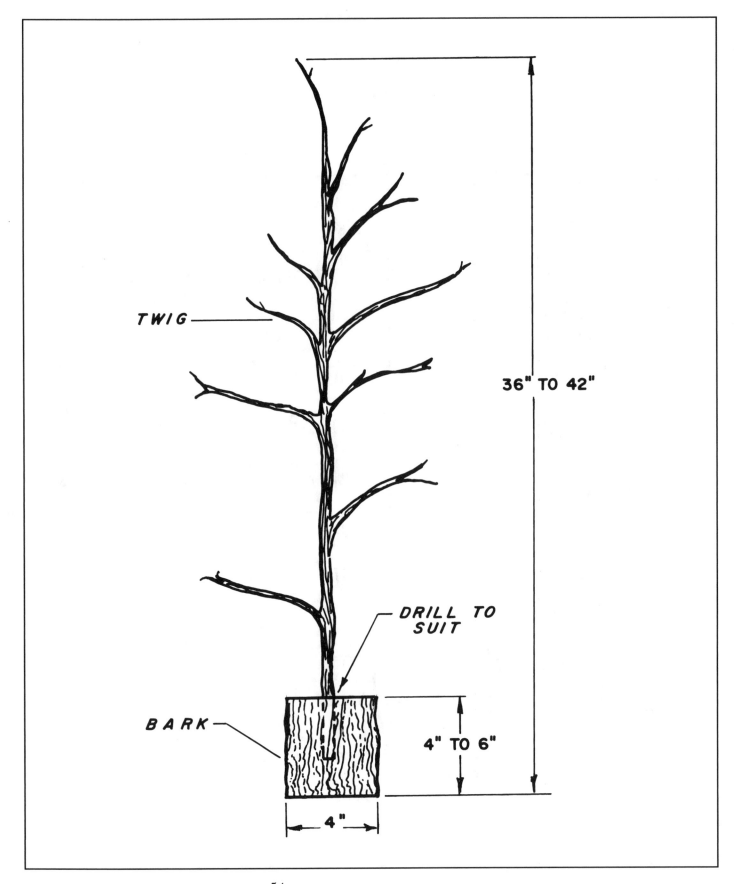

TWIG

BARK

DRILL TO SUIT

36" TO 42"

4" TO 6"

4"

Gingerbread Patriots

Add a patriotic touch to your 4th of July buffet table with a gingerbread boy and girl.

MATERIALS:
1/2-inch to 3/4-inch pine scraps, sandpaper, artist acrylic paint, stain, varnish.

TOOLS:
Band or scroll saw.

METHOD:
1. Transfer pattern to wood.
2. Cut out, sand all surfaces. You may stack 2 or 3 together.
3. With a pencil, sketch shirt, pants, blouse, skirt, star, stripes.
4. Paint face, hands, feet light gray; shirt and blouse, liberty blue; stripes on pants and skirt, red and ivory. Paint star ivory. Paint sides of wood to match front.
5. Apply walnut stain to back.
6. When dry, finish with clear satin varnish.
7. Tie baling twine around necks of figures.

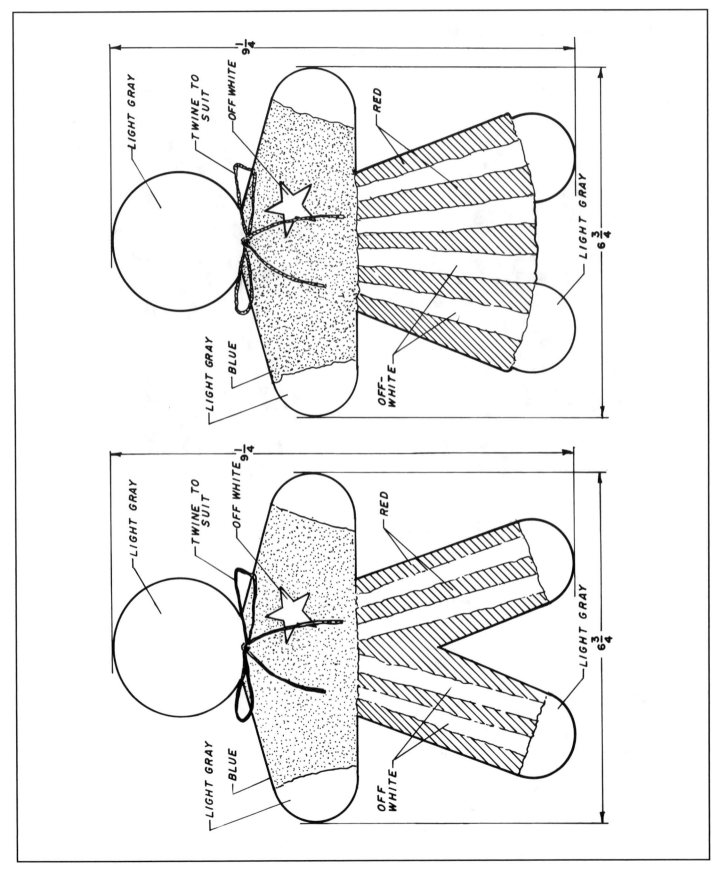

56

Uncle Sam

Here's a universal symbol with which to celebrate the nation's independence. What's more, the bigger you make him, the better he looks!

MATERIALS:

¼-inch and ½-inch scrap wood, 3/16-inch-diameter dowel, ⅛-inch-diameter dowel, rubber cement, paper or cloth flag, sand-paper, artist acrylic paint, walnut stain, tack rag, clear satin varnish.

TOOLS:

Scroll saw, drill.

METHOD:

1. Copy patterns and affix to wood with rubber cement.
2. Cut out body, arms, legs. Before removing patterns, drill all holes.
3. Remove patterns; lightly sand all parts.
4. Sketch Uncle Sam's details onto wood as shown. Both sides of each piece will be painted.
5. Paint face and hands a skin color. Beard, hair, stars, pole, and stripes are antique white. Eye is outlined with liner brush and black paint. Paint inside of outlined eye white, then add black dot for pupil. Mouth is colored with watered-down black paint.
6. Paint coat, hat brim, flag with liberty blue. Shoes are black.
7. Let dry. For an old, worn look, sand through paint on some edges. Wipe off any excess dust with tack rag. Wipe on walnut stain and remove immediately.
8. Make flag out of heavy paper and paint or buy one in a hobby shop.
9. When figure and flag are dry, apply varnish.
10. Glue flag to pole.
11. Glue ⅛-inch dowels to arms and legs, but not body. This will allow arms and legs to move slightly.

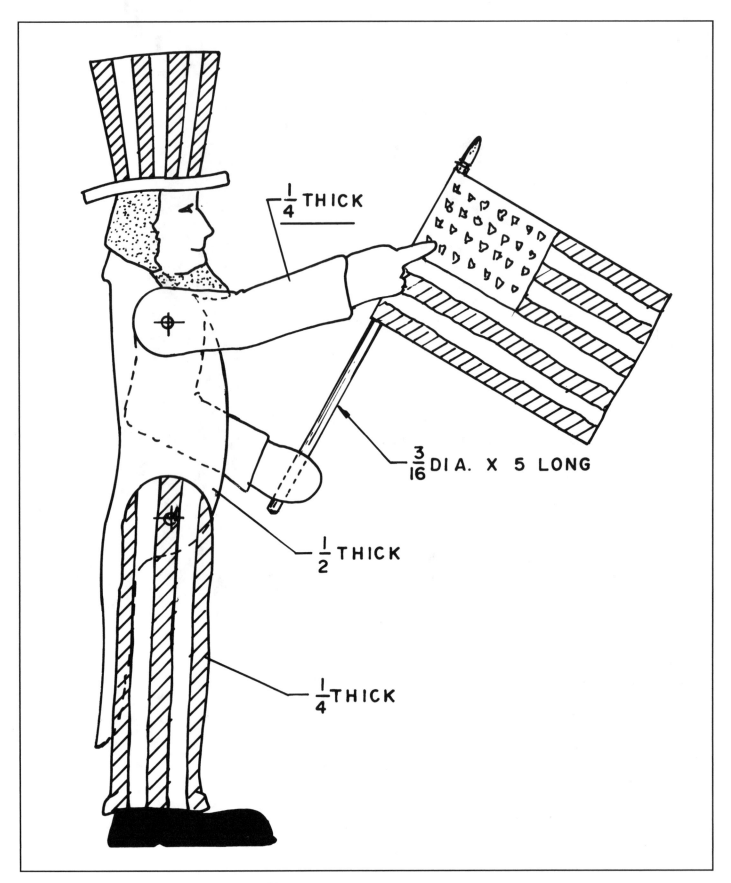

$\frac{1}{4}$ THICK

$\frac{3}{16}$ DIA. X 5 LONG

$\frac{1}{2}$ THICK

$\frac{1}{4}$ THICK

58

Flag of Independence

This project really brings on the spirit of patriotism. What could be simpler than a flag painted on a block of wood?

MATERIALS:
6-by-9-inch scrap of ³/4-inch pine, sandpaper, artist acrylic paint, No. 2 liner brush, walnut stain, clear satin varnish.

TOOLS:
Hand saw.

METHOD:
1. Cut board to size, slightly round edges, and sand.
2. Prime both sides.
3. Paint front ivory.
4. Lay out flag design with a pencil. This does not have to be perfect.
5. Paint field liberty blue and red stripes red iron oxide.
6. For antique look, sand edges slightly in some areas and down to bare wood in others.
7. Apply walnut stain and wipe off immediately. This will darken whole flag and give an antique look.
8. Apply top coat of clear satin varnish.

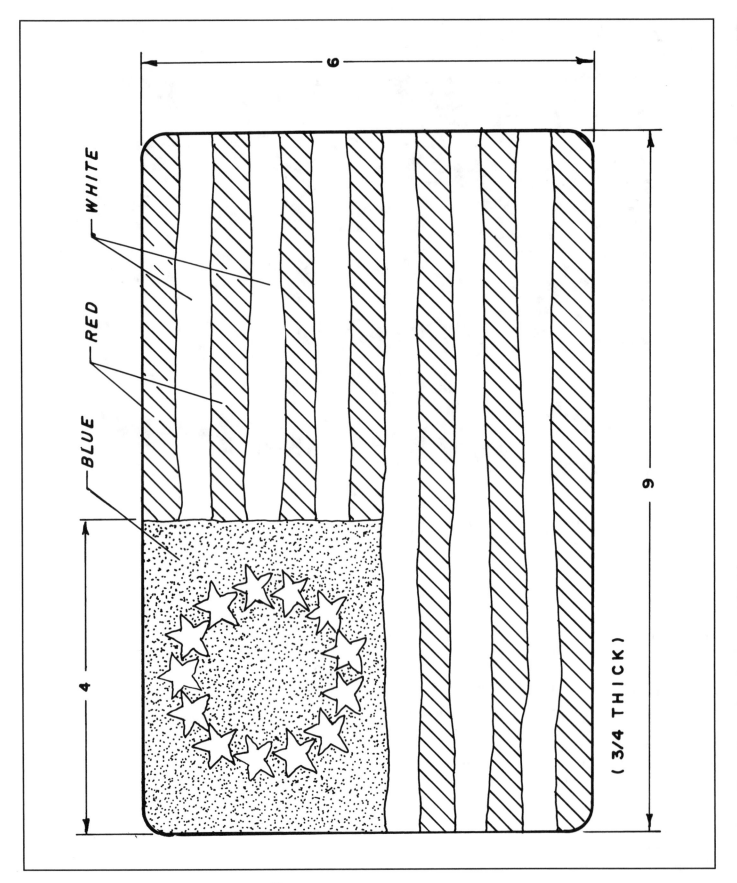

6

9

4

WHITE

RED

BLUE

(3/4 THICK)

Horse on Wheels (Red, White, and Blue)

This antique-looking project harks back to a time when Independence Day was a much more significant holiday than it is now. Hang it on a wall or put it on the fireplace mantle.

MATERIALS:

1/2-inch or 3/4-inch pine, two 2-inch pewter wheels, 2 brads or tacks, sandpaper, paint, varnish, artist acrylic paint, metallic brass paint, walnut stain, clear satin varnish.

TOOLS:

Scroll or band saw, hammer.

METHOD:

1. Lay out full-size pattern on heavy paper with a 1/2-inch grid.
2. Cut out; sand all surfaces.
3. Prime; resand lightly.
4. Paint front and sides ivory white. Let dry.
5. In pencil, draw mane, harness, harness rings, eye, mouth, and saddle.
6. Paint mane, tail, hooves midnight blue, harness and saddle maroon, harness rings with metallic brass. Eye and mouth are black.
7. When dry, sand lightly and apply light coat of walnut stain. Immediately rub off.
8. When dry, apply top coat of clear satin varnish.
9. Attach wheels with brads or tacks.

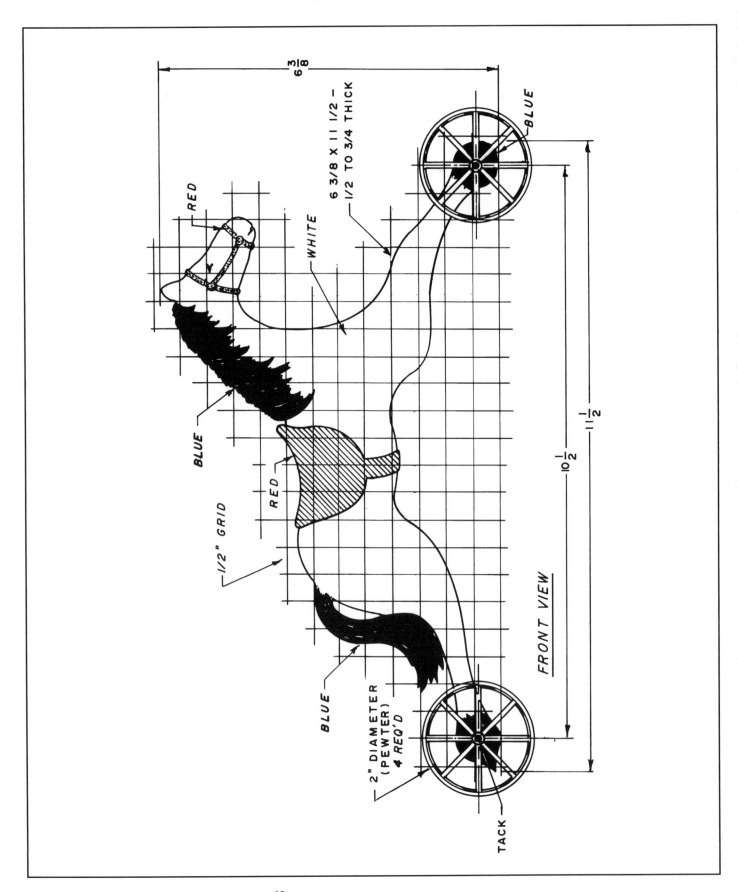

RED

BLUE

6 3/8

6 3/8 X 11 1/2 –
1/2 TO 3/4 THICK

WHITE

RED

BLUE

1/2" GRID

RED

BLUE

11 1/2

10 1/2

FRONT VIEW

2" DIAMETER
(PEWTER)
4 REQ'D

BLUE

TACK

Birdhouse
(Red, White, and Blue)

This birdhouse will add a patriotic touch to your family room or porch.

MATERIALS:

¹/₂-inch pine, ¹/₄-by-1³/₄-inch strips, ¹/₄-inch dowel, finishing nails, paint, varnish.

TOOLS:

Saw, drill, hammer, plane.

METHOD:

1. Cut all parts to size and shape. Lay out gable end of front and back walls on ¹/₂-inch grid. Front and back should be cut while attached so they're an exact pair.
2. Locate and drill 2-inch and ¹/₄-inch holes in front board.
3. "Round" front edges of roof with hand plane. These ten pieces are ¹/₄ inch thick by 1³/₄ inches wide and 6³/₄ inchs long.
4. Cut top edges of end pieces at 40 degrees so they will line up front and back.
5. Assemble front, back, end, and bottom with finishing nails. "Round" edges with hand plane as shown.
6. Attach roof pieces.
7. Prime all surfaces.
8. Lightly sand; paint antique white.
9. Carefully lay out red stripes ³/₄ inch apart. Paint burgundy rose.
10. Paint roof liberty blue.
11. When dry, add coat of waterproof varnish for outdoor use. For inside, use clear satin acrylic varnish.

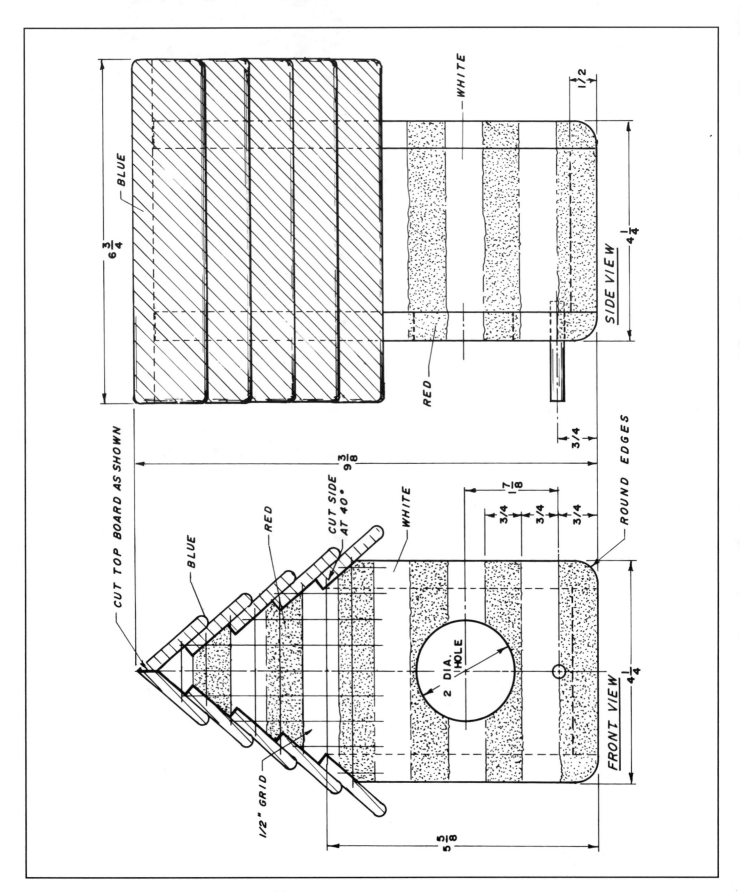

BLUE

$6\frac{3}{4}$

WHITE

$\frac{1}{2}$

$4\frac{1}{4}$

RED

SIDE VIEW

$3/4$

CUT TOP BOARD AS SHOWN

$9\frac{3}{8}$

BLUE

RED

CUT SIDE AT 40°

WHITE

ROUND EDGES

$1\frac{7}{8}$

$3/4$ $3/4$ $3/4$

$4\frac{1}{4}$

2 DIA. HOLE

FRONT VIEW

1/2" GRID

$5\frac{5}{8}$

Large Watermelon
Small Watermelon

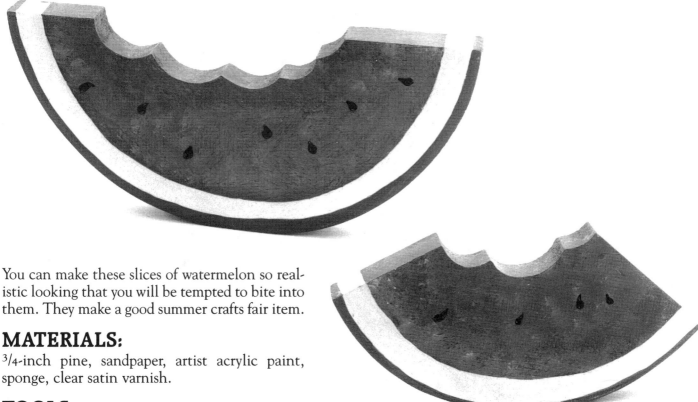

You can make these slices of watermelon so real-istic looking that you will be tempted to bite into them. They make a good summer crafts fair item.

MATERIALS:

3/4-inch pine, sandpaper, artist acrylic paint, sponge, clear satin varnish.

TOOLS:

Band or scroll saw, compass.

METHOD:

1. With compass, swing a 5 1/8-inch radius for outside edge. Make slices as drawn or as you please. No two have to be the same.
2. Lay out random "bites."
3. Prime all surfaces; lightly sand.
4. Sand a small flat spot on bottom edge so slice won't roll.
5. Paint all surfaces red.
6. Mark green and white sections with pencil.
7. Paint rind on both sides off-white.
8. Paint green outer section, letting it lap over into white about 1/16 inch as shown.
9. Pick up a little red and a little white paint on sponge and paint red section, making sure not to touch rind section. If you do, wipe off immediately. This gives watermelon a realistic look and shading.
10. Draw seeds in watermelon at random. Paint black. When dry, use light ivory for shading on seeds.
11. Finish with clear satin varnish.

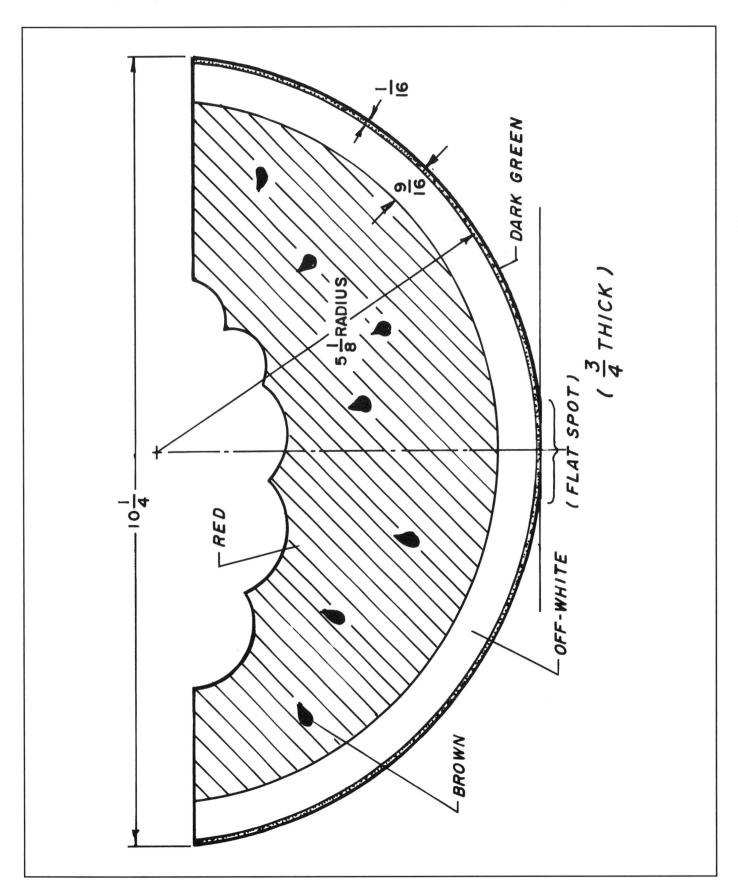

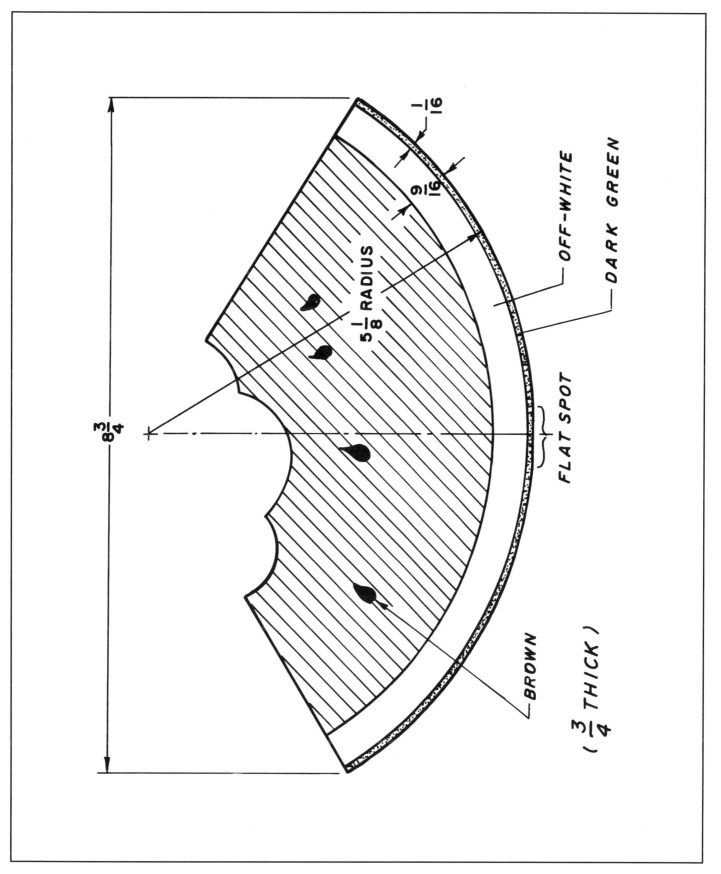

Wheelbarrow

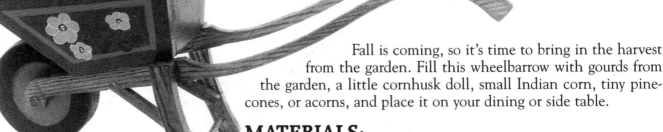

Fall is coming, so it's time to bring in the harvest from the garden. Fill this wheelbarrow with gourds from the garden, a little cornhusk doll, small Indian corn, tiny pinecones, or acorns, and place it on your dining or side table.

MATERIALS:

1/4-inch wood, 3/4-inch dowel, 1/16-inch wood, 3/16-inch dowel, 5/8-inch scrap wood, sandpaper, glue, paint, stain (optional), varnish.

TOOLS:

Saw, band saw, drill, rasp.

METHOD:

1. This is one of the more complicated projects in the book; before proceeding, study how each piece is made and how they go together.
2. Using thickness of wood noted for each part, lay out all parts on wood.
3. Cut out each piece. Make exact pairs of duplicate pieces.
4. Assemble front, back, and sides; sand all corners.
5. Make exact pair of handles. "Round" the section as shown. Drill 3/16-inch hole at an angle as shown.
6. Cut out legs, wheel, tires.
7. Assemble wheel and tires.
8. Assemble undercarriage with glue and temporarily add wheel with tires. Add spreader dowel.
9. Take wheel and tires off.
10. Paint all parts as noted.
11. With tracing paper, copy patterns of stripe and flower for both sides of wheelbarrow.
12. Rub chalk on back of traced patterns, then tape paper with pattern to appropriate side of wheelbarrow.
13. Trace pattern onto wheelbarrow. Remove paper; chalk outline of stripe and flowers are ready to paint.
14. Use No. 6 round brush to paint flowers. Start in center of one petal and pivot tip of brush until all petals are done. For centers of flowers, use wooden end of brush; dab into paint and dab a series of dots in a small circle.
15. Paint leaves and stems with little sweeping strokes.
16. Paint tire black.
17. Leave handle and undercarriage in natural wood color.
18. Finish all pieces with clear satin varnish.
19. Assemble wheel and axle; it should rotate freely.

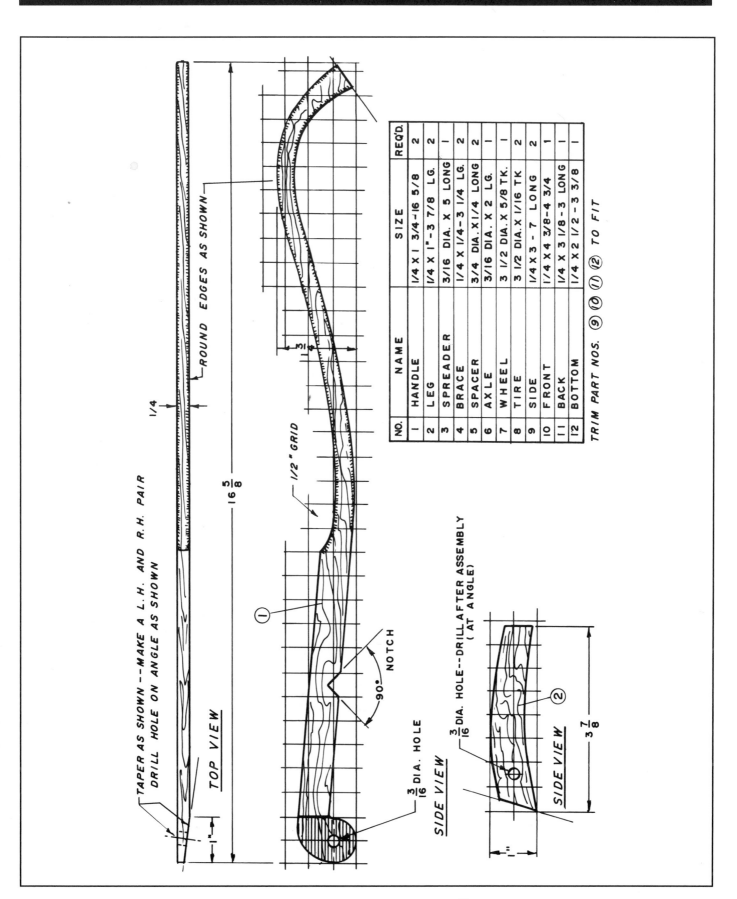

NO.	NAME	SIZE	REQ'D.
1	HANDLE	1/4 X 1 3/4-16 5/8	2
2	LEG	1/4 X 1"-3 7/8 LG.	2
3	SPREADER	3/16 DIA. X 5 LONG	1
4	BRACE	1/4 X 1/4-3 1/4 LG.	2
5	SPACER	3/4 DIA. X 1/4 LONG	2
6	AXLE	3/16 DIA. X 2 LG.	1
7	WHEEL	3 1/2 DIA. X 5/8 TK.	1
8	TIRE	3 1/2 DIA. X 1/16 TK	2
9	SIDE	1/4 X 3 - 7 LONG	2
10	FRONT	1/4 X 4 3/8-4 3/4	1
11	BACK	1/4 X 3 1/8-3 LONG	1
12	BOTTOM	1/4 X 2 1/2-3 3/8	1

TRIM PART NOS. ⑨ ⑩ ⑪ ⑫ TO FIT

TAPER AS SHOWN --MAKE A L.H. AND R.H. PAIR
DRILL HOLE ON ANGLE AS SHOWN

ROUND EDGES AS SHOWN

1/4

16 5/8

1/2" GRID

TOP VIEW

①

NOTCH

90°

3/16 DIA. HOLE

SIDE VIEW

3/16 DIA. HOLE--DRILL AFTER ASSEMBLY
(AT ANGLE)

②

3 7/8

SIDE VIEW

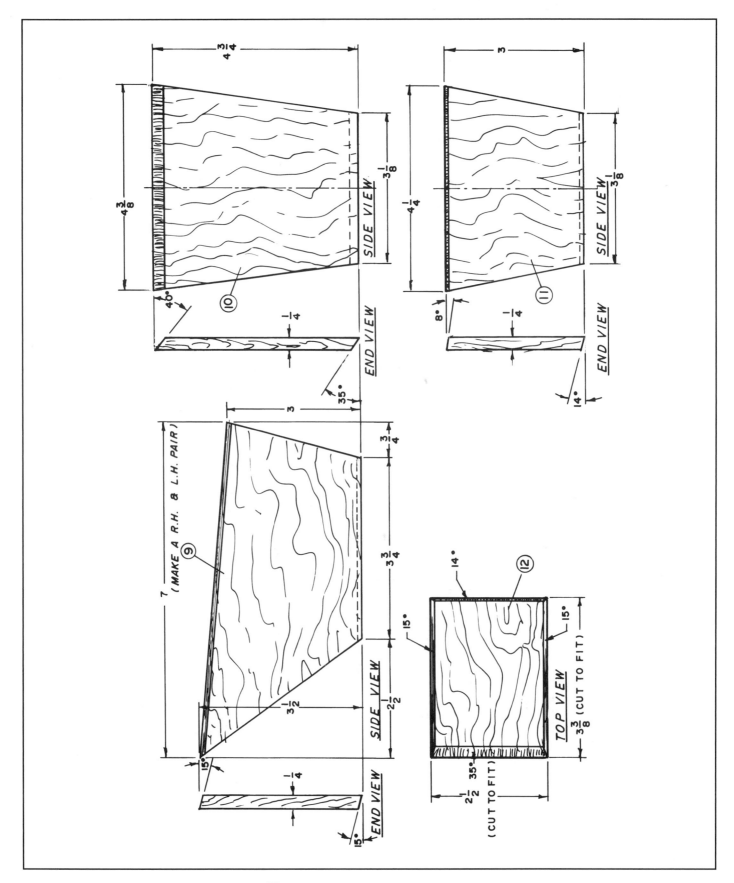

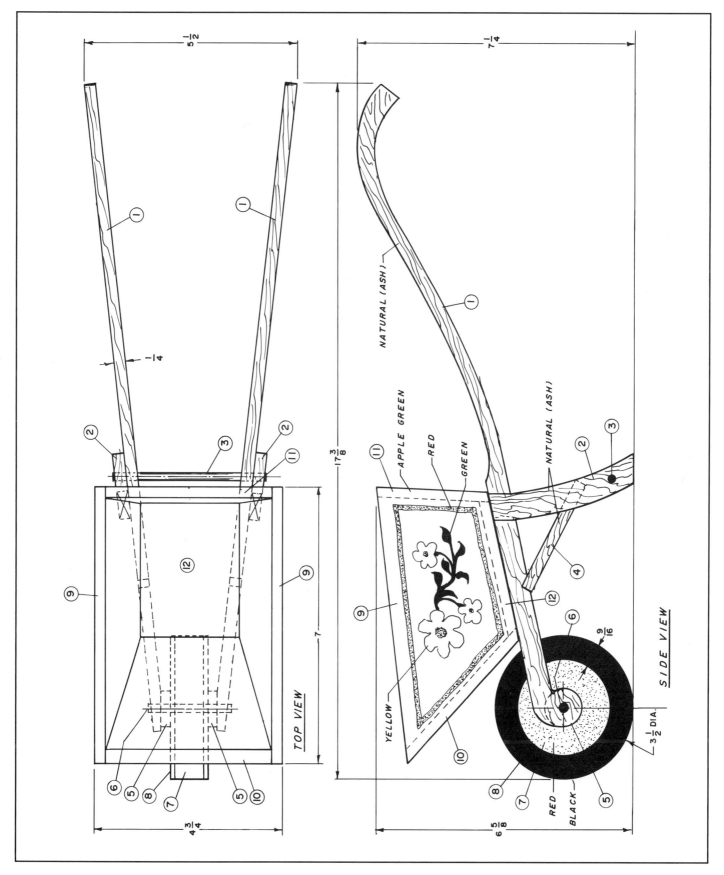

TOP VIEW

SIDE VIEW

$5\frac{1}{2}$

$\frac{1}{4}$

$4\frac{3}{4}$

7

$7\frac{1}{4}$

$17\frac{3}{8}$

$6\frac{5}{8}$

$3\frac{1}{2}$ DIA.

$\frac{9}{16}$

NATURAL (ASH)

NATURAL (ASH)

APPLE GREEN

RED

GREEN

YELLOW

RED

BLACK

Wagon

Here is another fall project to fill with gourds, Indian corn, bittersweet, or straw flowers.

MATERIALS:

¼-inch and miscellaneous scrap wood pieces, paint, glue, spray varnish, walnut stain, four 2½-inch pewter wheels, 4 tacks.

TOOLS:

Scroll saw, hand or table saw, hammer.

METHOD:

1. Cut all pieces to size according to cutting list. Most are square cuts.
2. Lay out and cut axle support according to detailed illustrations.
3. Glue axle supports to base, located in 1⅝ inches from each end so hubs of wheels will be 2 inches as noted.
4. Glue side rails to posts and end rails to ends to form a box.
5. Glue upright supports, seat, and seat back in place as shown.
6. Glue all to base assembly.
7. Fit rod to support with ¹⁄₁₆-inch-diameter pin (cut from coat hanger).
8. Add ⅛-inch dowel to rod to make front tee.
9. Glue pieces to base.
10. Paint wagon light gray. Seat, undercarriage, and handle are red.
11. For antique look, rub walnut stain over wagon and parts.
12. Spray wagon with clear varnish.
13. Add wheels.

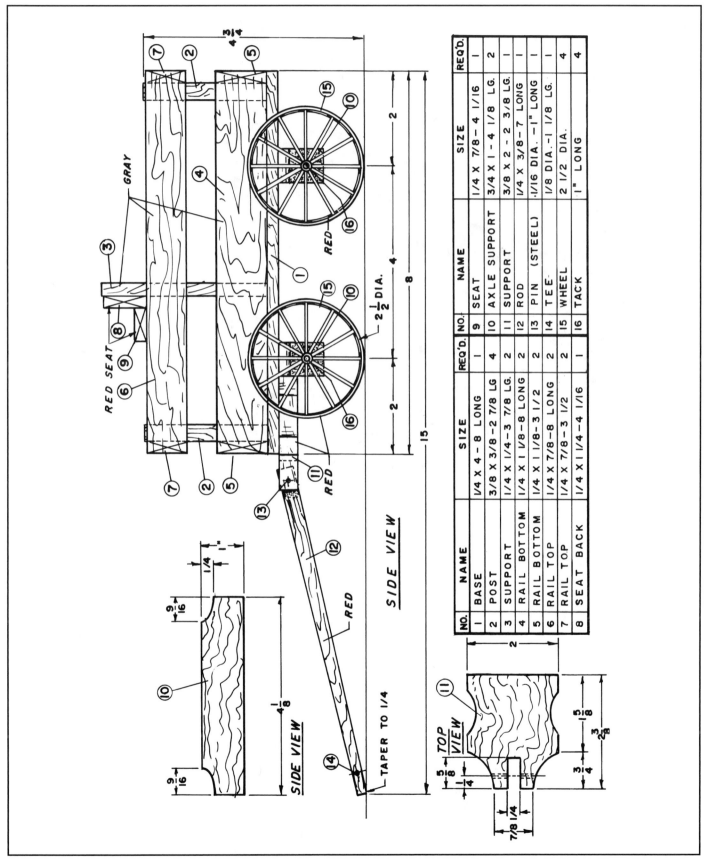

NO.	NAME	SIZE	REQ'D.
1	BASE	1/4 X 4 - 8 LONG	1
2	POST	3/8 X 3/8 - 2 7/8 LG	4
3	SUPPORT	1/4 X 1/4 - 3 7/8 LG.	2
4	RAIL BOTTOM	1/4 X 1 1/8 - 8 LONG	2
5	RAIL BOTTOM	1/4 X 1 1/8 - 3 1/2	2
6	RAIL TOP	1/4 X 7/8 - 8 LONG	2
7	RAIL TOP	1/4 X 7/8 - 3 1/2	2
8	SEAT BACK	1/4 X 1 1/4 - 4 1/16	1
9	SEAT	1/4 X 7/8 - 4 1/16	1
10	AXLE SUPPORT	3/4 X 1 - 4 1/8 LG.	2
11	SUPPORT	3/8 X 2 - 2 3/8 LG.	1
12	ROD	1/4 X 3/8 - 7 LONG	1
13	PIN (STEEL)	.1/16 DIA. - 1" LONG	1
14	TEE-	1/8 DIA. - 1 1/8 LG.	1
15	WHEEL	2 1/2 DIA.	4
16	TACK	1" LONG	4

SIDE VIEW

TOP VIEW

TAPER TO 1/4

Leaf Shelf

Here is a sign of fall that you do not have to rake up and bag. It makes a beautiful knickknack shelf.

MATERIALS:
¼-inch plywood, rubber cement, stain, sandpaper, varnish, brads.

TOOLS:
Scroll saw, hammer, drill.

METHOD:
1. Copy pattern and glue lightly to wood with rubber cement. Pattern for shelf itself is half-round (3¼-inch radius) and brace profile is shaped.
2. Cut out and sand pieces. Drill ⅛-inch hole.
3. Using small brads, tack shelf and brace in place from back.
4. Apply stain over all surfaces.
5. Add 2 or 3 coats clear varnish.

74

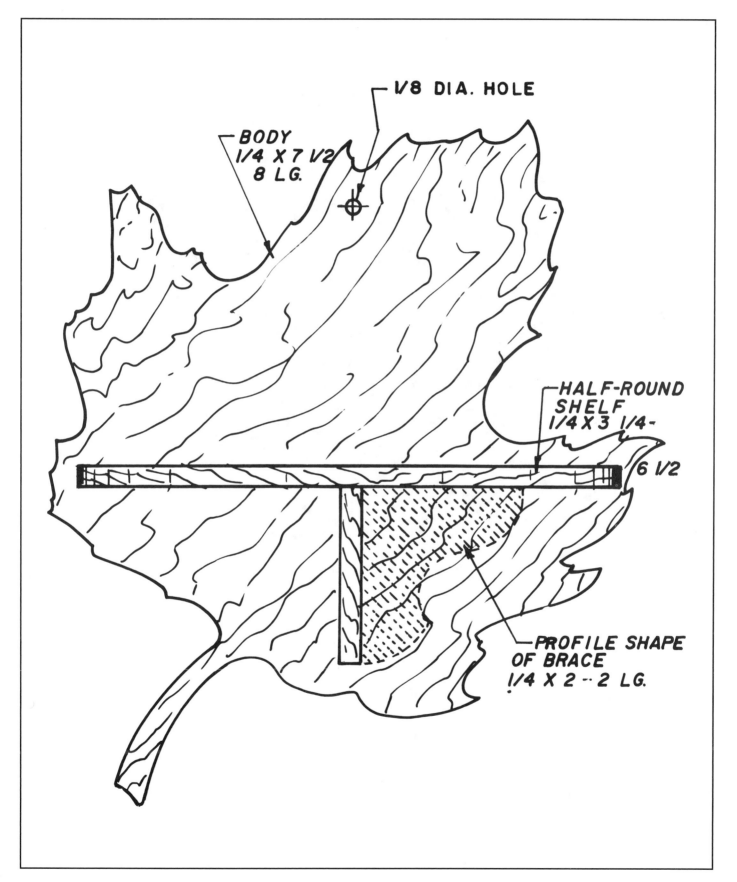

1/8 DIA. HOLE

BODY
1/4 X 7 1/2
8 LG.

HALF-ROUND
SHELF
1/4 X 3 1/4-

6 1/2

PROFILE SHAPE
OF BRACE
1/4 X 2 - 2 LG.

Leaf Napkin Holder

This is in keeping with the spirit of fall and uses the same pattern as the leaf shelf.

MATERIALS:

$1/4$-inch plywood, $1^5/8$-by-$6^3/4$-inch piece of $3/4$-inch scrap wood, sandpaper, glue, stain, varnish.

TOOLS:

Scroll saw, table saw.

METHOD:

1. Transfer full-size pattern to wood and temporarily attach 2 pieces of plywood with tape or small brads.
2. Cut out at same time so sides match exactly.
3. Cut base to size.
4. Glue sides to base as shown. Don't use too much glue.
5. Stain all surfaces; lightly sand.
6. Apply 2 or 3 coats of clear satin varnish.

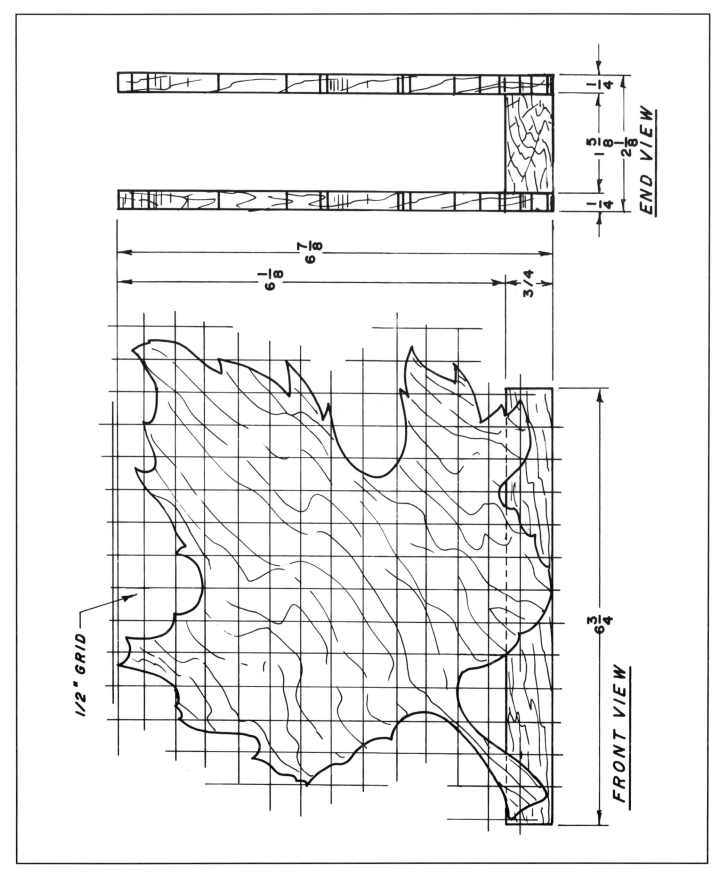

1/2" GRID

END VIEW

$\frac{1}{4}$

$5\frac{5}{8}$ $2\frac{1}{8}$

$\frac{1}{4}$

$6\frac{7}{8}$

$6\frac{1}{8}$

3/4

$6\frac{3}{4}$

FRONT VIEW

An Apple for the Teacher

September brings the first day of school. This project will make a nice back-to-school gift for your child's teacher or simply remind you of your old school days.

MATERIALS:

½-inch wood, twine, brads, scrap wood, ¼- to ⅜-inch-thick scraps, sandpaper, paint, varnish.

TOOLS:

Scroll saw, band saw, hammer.

METHOD:

1. Transfer pattern of apple to ½-inch-thick piece of wood and cut out. Sand all surfaces.
2. Shelf is a half-round of ½-inch-thick wood, 1⅞-inch radius.
3. Nail shelf to apple.
4. Cut the books from scrap wood: ½-by-3-by-3½ inches, ⅜-by-2¼-by-2¾ inches, ¼-by-1½-by-2¼ inches.
5. Optional: Slightly round left side of each book with sandpaper to simulate roundness of binding.
6. Mix brown and red paint to make brick color for apple and shelf.
7. Paint leaves green and stem brown.
8. Paint books yellow, red, and blue. When dry, paint top, bottom, right side antique white to simulate paper.
9. When white is dry, thin out burnt umber. Pick up mixture on tip of brush and lightly pull over antique white to simulate page edges.
10. With soft pencil, sketch ABCs on small book. Paint letters antique white.
11. Tie books together with twine and place on shelf.

78

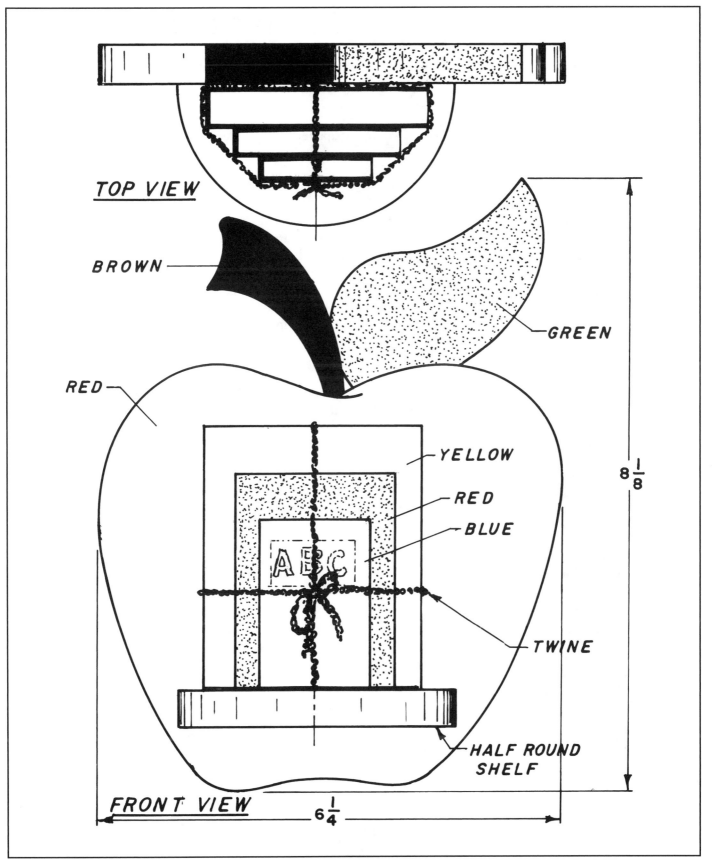

TOP VIEW

BROWN

GREEN

RED

YELLOW

RED

BLUE

ABC

TWINE

HALF ROUND
SHELF

$8\frac{1}{8}$

FRONT VIEW

$6\frac{1}{4}$

Six Apples on a String

Here in New Hampshire, fall is apple-picking time. This project will keep the apple harvest in your mind all through the winter months.

MATERIALS:

3/4-inch wood, sandpaper, primer, paint, varnish, twine.

TOOLS:

Band or scroll saw, drill.

METHOD:

1. Transfer apple patterns to wood.
2. Cut out; sand all surfaces.
3. Mix brown and red paint, but not too thoroughly. This creates a simple yet effective shading on apples.
4. Paint stems brown and shade with black.
5. Leaves are green with light green and white for shading. When dry, finish leaves with a little black paint for shading and draw veins.
6. Paint "bites" out of apples an off-white.
7. Draw seeds on appropriate apples, paint black, and highlight with a little yellow. Look at drawing of apples before decorating them.
8. Finish apples with clear satin varnish.
9. Tie apples together with twine and hang them.

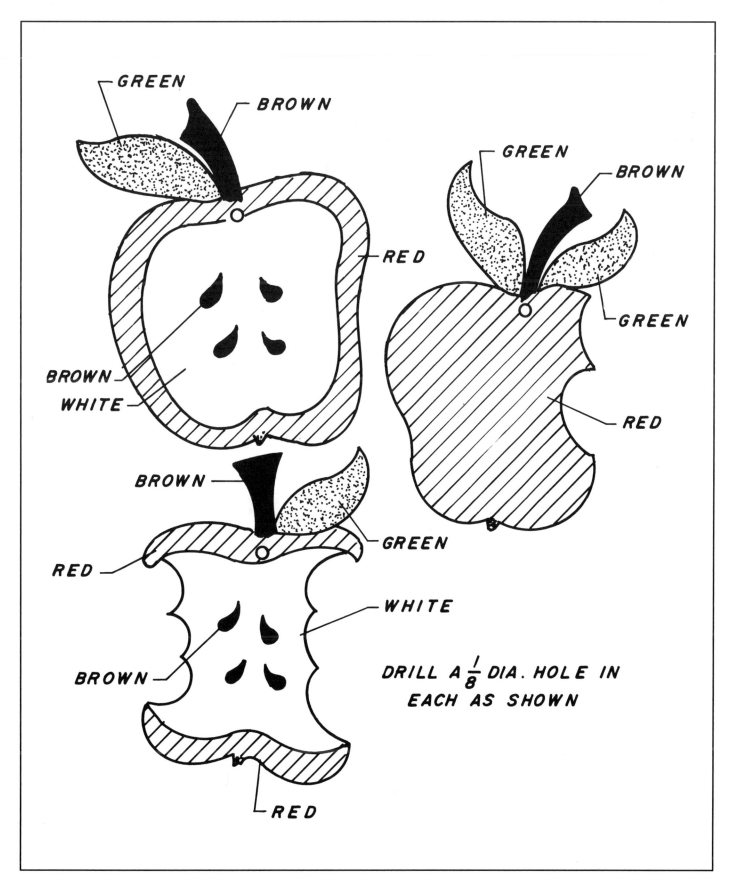

GREEN

BROWN

GREEN

BROWN

RED

GREEN

RED

BROWN

WHITE

BROWN

RED

GREEN

WHITE

BROWN

DRILL A $\frac{1}{8}$ DIA. HOLE IN EACH AS SHOWN

RED

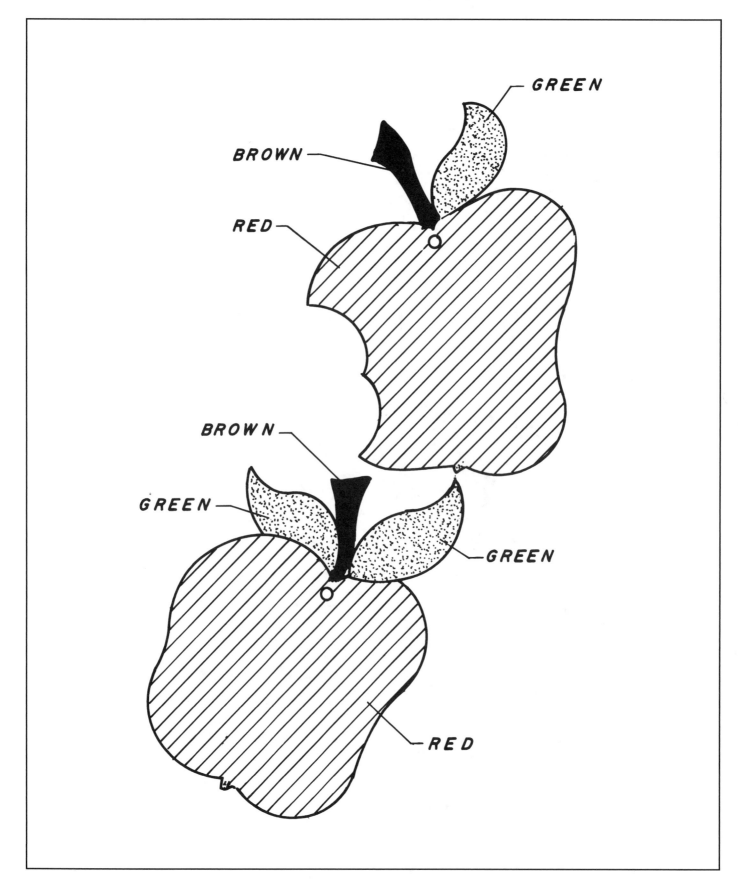

Scary Black Cat

This is a copy of a design used years ago. It will add a special touch nestled among 2 or 3 pumpkins in your Halloween display.

MATERIALS:
³⁄₈-inch to ¹⁄₂-inch wood, sandpaper, paint, varnish.

TOOLS:
Band or scroll saw.

METHOD:
1. Transfer pattern to wood and cut out.
2. Prime and paint all surfaces black.
3. Paint cat's collar orange.
4. Finish with clear varnish.

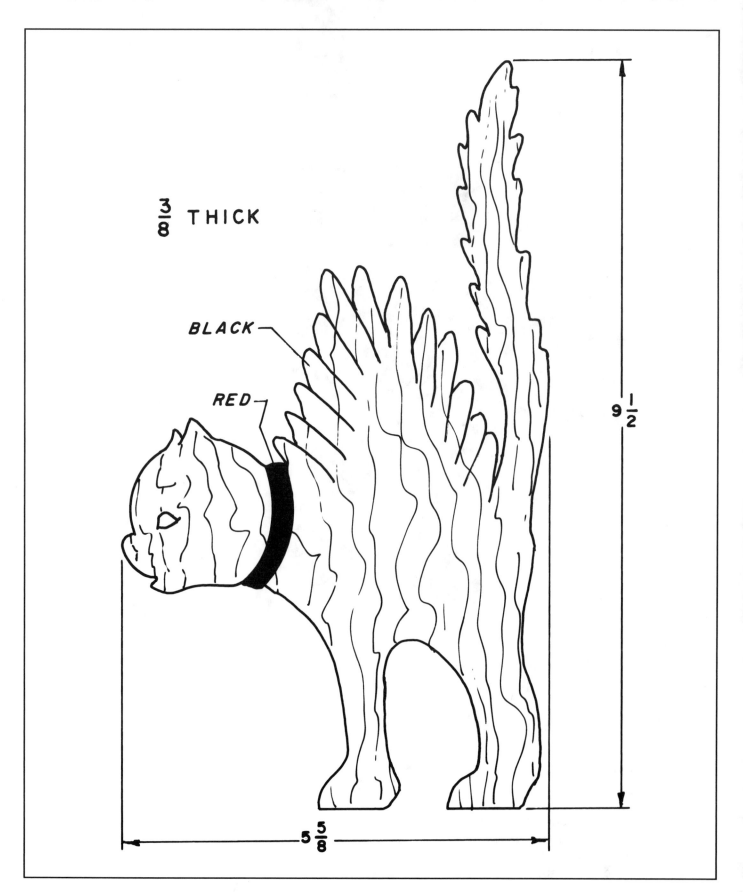

$\frac{3}{8}$ THICK

BLACK

RED

$9\frac{1}{2}$

$5\frac{5}{8}$

Black Cat on Wheels

Try this unusual Halloween project. After all, how often do you see a cat on wheels?

MATERIALS:

3/4-inch pine, 1/2-inch pine, 1 1/2-inch dowels for wheels (cut 3/8 inch thick), 3/16-inch dowel, paint, varnish.

TOOLS:

Scroll or band saw, drill, sandpaper.

METHOD:

1. Transfer pattern to wood and cut out.
2. Make base 1/2 inch thick, 2 inches wide, and 6 3/8 inches long.
3. Make 2 axle supports about 3/8 inch thick by 1/2 inch wide and 2 inches long. Make a saw kerf (slot) 3/16 inch square along top edge to support axles.
4. Glue cat and axle supports to base (kerf on top).
5. Cut wheels from 1 1/2-inch dowel about 3/8 inch thick; drill 3/16-inch hole through each.
6. Prime all pieces. When dry, paint cat black, base orange, wheels black, ribbon orange.
7. Cut 2 axles 3 inches long. Prime and paint these orange. When dry, insert them into kerf in axle supports.
8. Glue wheels to axles; they must turn freely.
9. Varnish all pieces.

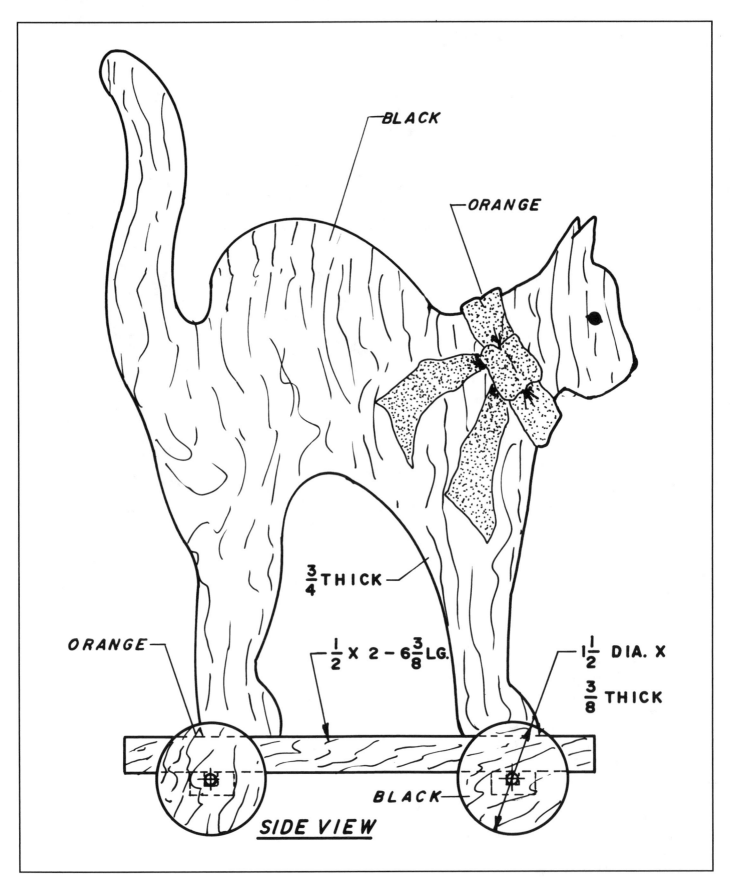

BLACK

ORANGE

$\frac{3}{4}$ THICK

ORANGE

$\frac{1}{2}$ X 2 - 6$\frac{3}{8}$ LG.

$1\frac{1}{2}$ DIA. X $\frac{3}{8}$ THICK

BLACK

SIDE VIEW

Witch on a Broom

This Halloween witch may be made to any size by using larger grids. Try placing it on top of a cupboard or hanging it on a wall.

MATERIALS:
1/4-inch to 3/8-inch wood, sandpaper, primer, paint, gloss varnish.

TOOLS:
Scroll saw.

METHOD:
1. Transfer pattern to wood and cut out.
2. Prime. When dry, paint black on all surfaces.
3. Apply top coat of gloss varnish.

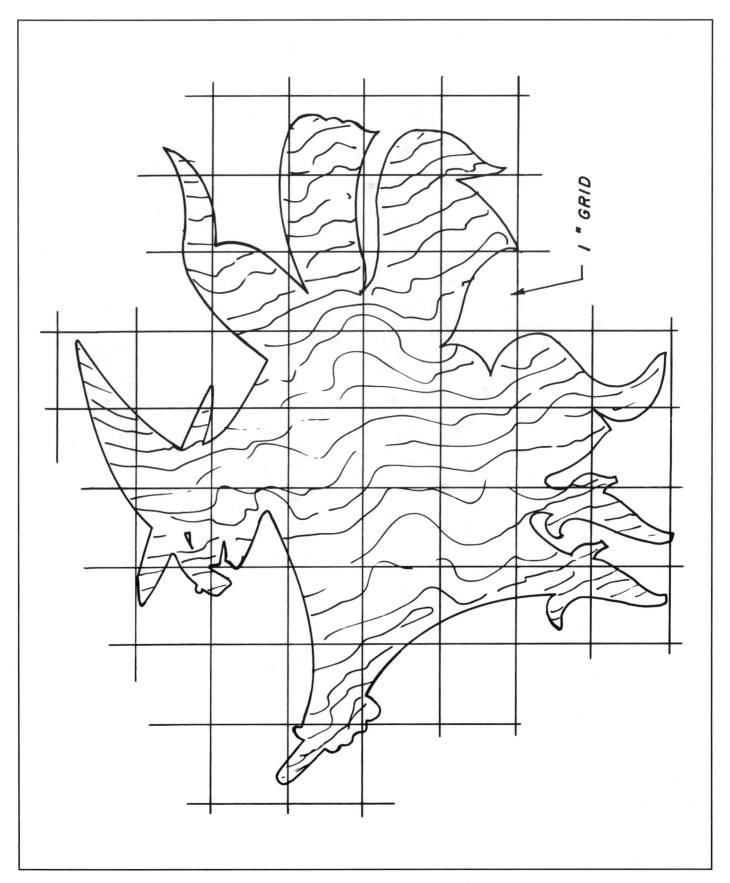

I " GRID

The Witch's Brew

I found this pattern in an antique shop. I'd say it went back 50 years or so. It was hand cut and somewhat crude, and inspired an unusual Halloween project. Perhaps yours will be around for the next 50 years.

MATERIALS:
1/2-inch pine, sandpaper, primer, paint, varnish.

TOOLS:
Scroll saw, drill.

METHOD:
1. Using 1-inch grid, make a full-size pattern.
2. Transfer pattern to wood and cut out.
3. Prime and paint all surfaces black. All openings and saw cuts must be painted.
4. Inside of cat's eyes, flames, jack-o'-lantern are painted orange.
5. Paint stem of jack-o'-lantern green with brown shading and growth lines.
6. Paint broom brown.
7. Paint witch's face, arms, hands, and leg ivory.
8. When dry, finish with a coat of gloss varnish.

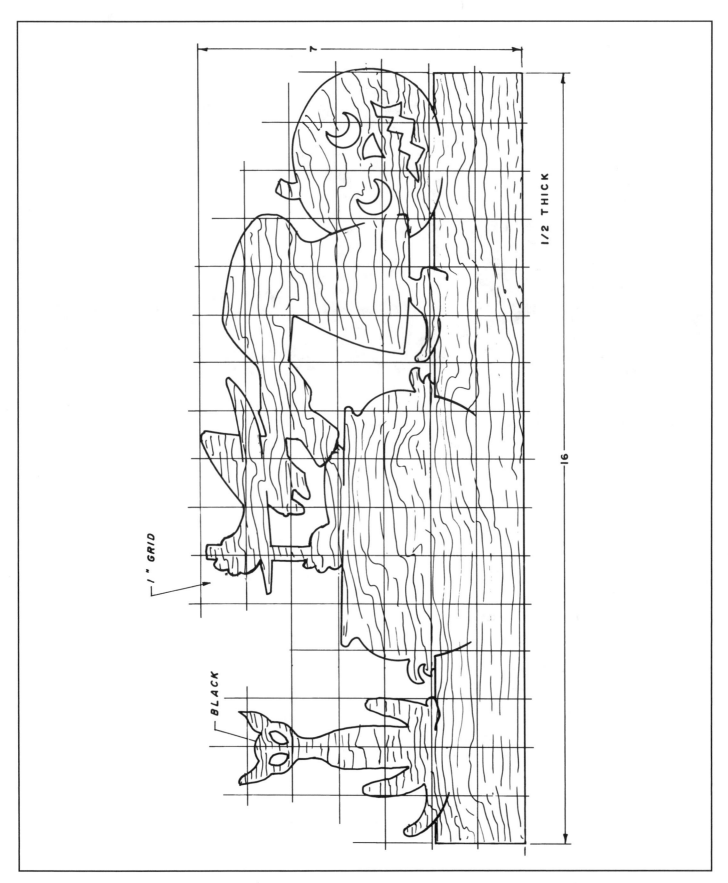

Jack-o'-Lantern
with Candle Holder

What do you think of at Halloween? A jack-o'-lantern, of course. Here is one you can use year after year. This one uses a candle but a small electric light could be substituted.

MATERIALS:
³/4-inch wood, candle holder, candle or light fixture, sandpaper, paint, varnish, finishing nails.

TOOLS:
Scroll saw, drill, hammer.

METHOD:
1. Carefully lay out two full-size patterns using a 1-inch grid (one is for jack-o'-lantern, one for grass).
2. Transfer pattern to wood and cut out.
3. Cut base ³/4 inch thick, 2¹/2 inches wide, and 6 inches long.
4. Glue and nail grass to jack-o'-lantern; nail and glue base to jack-o'-lantern and grass.
5. Attach candle holder to base behind jack-o'-lantern; refer to drawing.
6. Paint jack-o'-lantern orange; cover interior edges of eyes, nose, and mouth.
7. For shading and a look of roundness, use a darker orange and paint curves with long, flowing strokes.
8. When dry, load one side of paintbrush with orange and the other with brown; use long, sweeping strokes over or near darker orange strokes to give more shading.
9. Paint grass green. Use brown for shading and liner brush for highlighting.
10. When dry, finish with clear varnish.

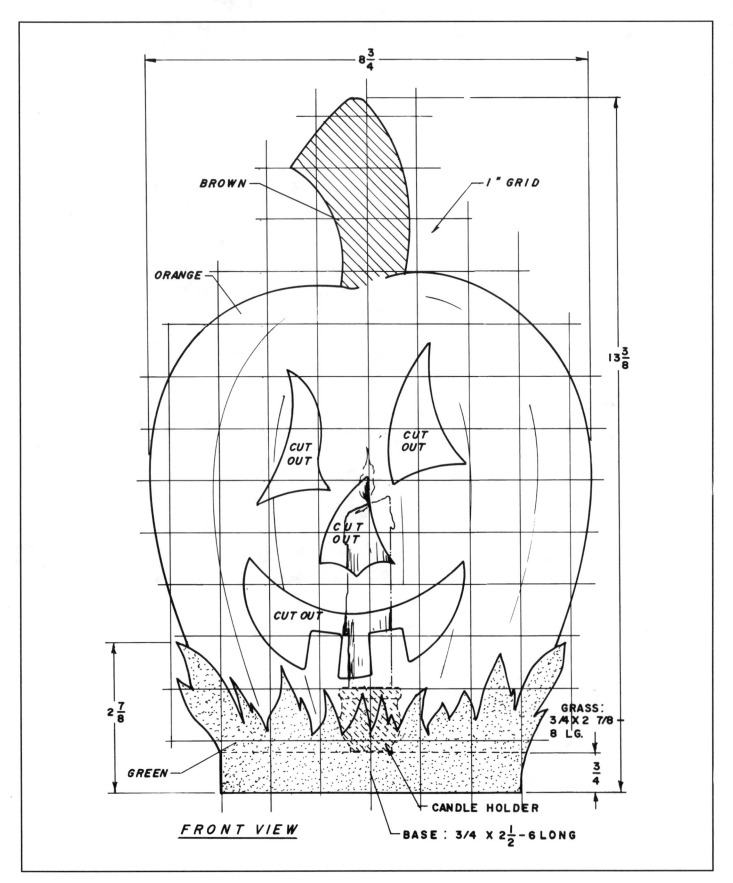

BROWN

ORANGE

1" GRID

8 3/4

13 3/8

CUT OUT

CUT OUT

CUT OUT

CUT OUT

2 7/8

GRASS:
3/4 X 2 7/8 -
8 LG.

3/4

GREEN

CANDLE HOLDER

BASE : 3/4 X 2 1/2 - 6 LONG

FRONT VIEW

Donkey and Elephant

I live in New Hampshire, which has the presidential primary, so we usually have the candidates here longer than anyplace else. This donkey and elephant will grace your house anytime there's a political campaign.

MATERIALS:

Wood scraps (¹/₄ to ³/₈ inch thick), artist acrylic paint, varnish.

METHOD:

1. Copy pattern and transfer to wood.
2. Cut out; sand lightly.
3. Paint both light gray.
4. With soft pencil, add details on donkey and elephant, as illustrated.
5. Paint liberty blue, antique white, and red iron oxide.
6. Finish with clear satin varnish.

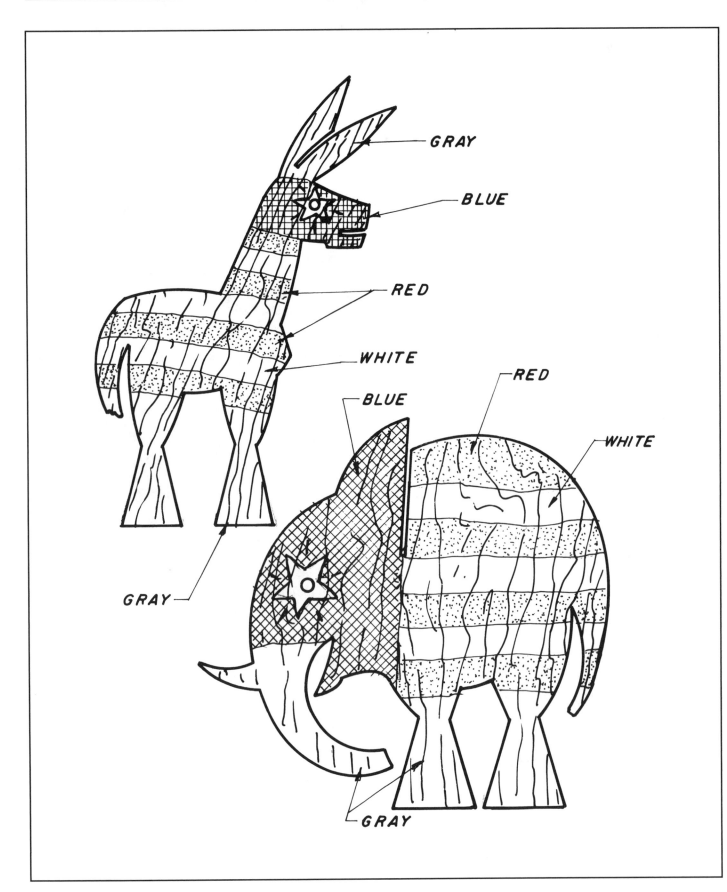

Turkey Candelabra

What better centerpiece could you have for Thanksgiving? It will add a festive look to any table along with flowers, gourds, or pumpkins.

MATERIALS:
3/4-inch wood, 5/8-inch wood, 3 candles 5/8 inch wide, paint, No. 1 and No. 2 paintbrushes, sponge, varnish.

TOOLS:
Scroll or band saw, drill or drill press.

METHOD:
1. Using a 1/2-inch grid, make full-size pattern of turkey and base.
2. Transfer patterns to wood and cut out. Sand lightly.
3. Locate and drill three 5/8-inch-diameter holes for candles. Holes must run in straight line.
4. Glue turkey to base.
5. Paint turkey and base gray.
6. Sponge paint turkey body with mixture of brown iron oxide and black. Use overlapping strokes to get look of feathers. When dry, use No. 1 brush to highlight and make quills in the feathers with a Georgia clay paint. (Use photo of a turkey for more detail of feathers).
7. After this dries, outline tips of feathers here and there with ivory paint.
8. Sponge paint tip of head with Georgia clay paint.
9. Before this dries, take a sponge and dab all over this area with a circular motion.
10. After this dries, use No. 2 brush and dab Georgia clay paint over same area. This gives depth and realism to turkey.
11. Paint hole of eye with Georgia clay. Next outline eye, around head, and below head with mixture of brown iron oxide and black.
12. Paint tiny part of face, near eye, with watered-down spruce blue. This gives the bluish color of turkey's face.
13. Paint legs and feet with thinned-out Georgia clay. When dry, use black and brown iron oxide mixture to outline legs and feet.
14. Finish with clear satin varnish.
15. Adjust holes so that candles fit correctly.

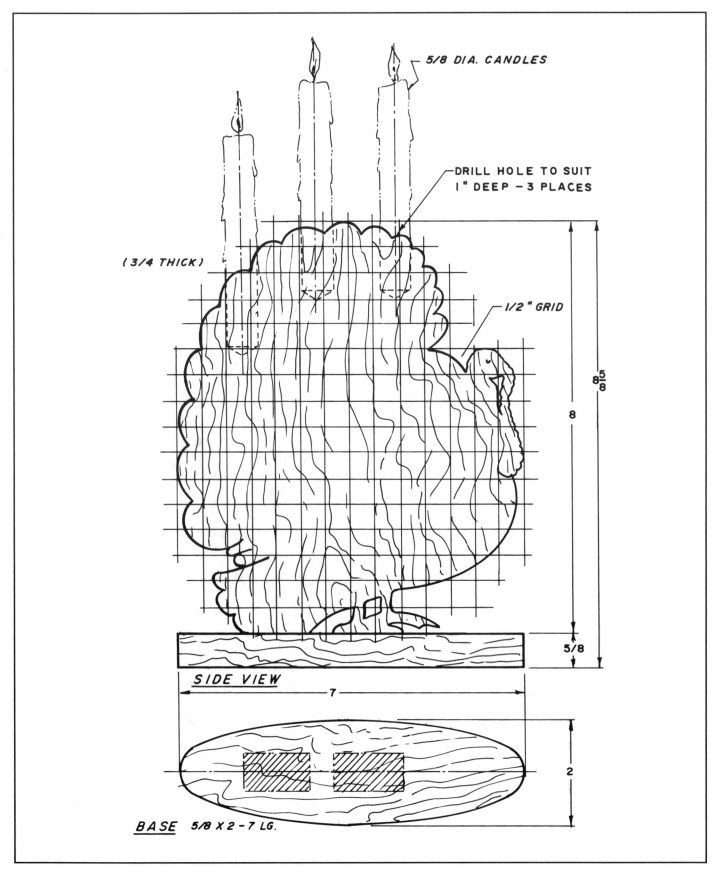

5/8 DIA. CANDLES

DRILL HOLE TO SUIT
1" DEEP – 3 PLACES

(3/4 THICK)

1/2" GRID

$8\frac{5}{8}$

8

5/8

SIDE VIEW

7

2

BASE 5/8 X 2 - 7 LG.

Turkey

A turkey-shaped cutting board works well because of the round body shape. You also can use it as a hot pad or trivet if you want.

MATERIALS:
3/4-inch to 1-inch hardwood, sandpaper, vegetable oil.

TOOLS:
Scroll or band saw.

METHOD:
1. Draw turkey full-size using 1-inch grid.
2. Transfer pattern to wood and cut out.
3. Sand all surfaces.
4. Rub wood with vegetable oil.

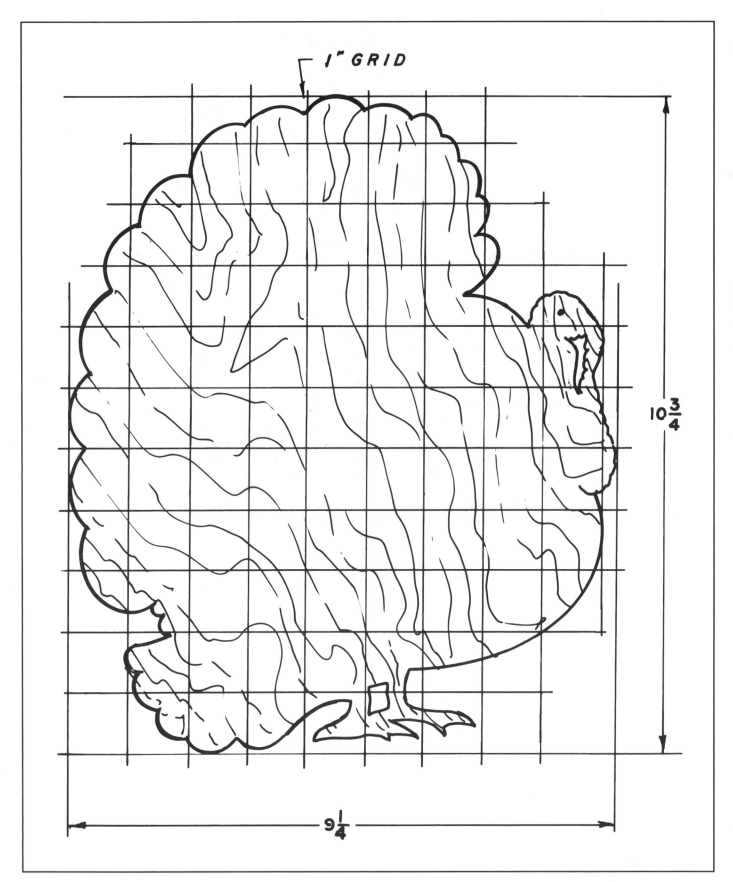

1" GRID

$10\frac{3}{4}$

$9\frac{1}{4}$

Pilgrims

Here are charming decorations that your children or grandchildren will enjoy around Thanksgiving.

MATERIALS:
1/2-inch to 3/4-inch scrap wood, artist acrylic paint, rubber cement, varnish.

TOOLS:
Scroll or band saw.

METHOD:
1. Make copy of pattern and cement to wood.
2. Cut out.
3. Remove pattern and sand lightly.
4. Prime.
5. With soft pencil, sketch details of Pilgrims.
6. Paint dress, suit, hat, bonnet a gray color. Collars, cuffs, socks, apron are white and highlighted with grayish black. Make sure to carry paint over onto edges.
7. Paint ribbons on hat and hatband, as well as shoes, black.
8. Paint hat buckle silver; hair on both burnt umber with a touch of golden brown.
9. Paint hands, face a flesh color with cheeks, mouth, and hands outlined in adobe.
10. To finish, outline eyebrows, eyes, nose in black. Use white paint for eyeballs, with a small dot of black for pupils.
11. Finish with clear satin varnish.

8

3

3 1/4

(1/2 THICK)

Snowman

This fun project can be made from a flat ³/₄-inch piece of wood (as shown) or it may be turned on a lathe for a 3-dimensional effect. Either way, it will enrich your winter decorations.

MATERIALS:

³/₄-inch board or 3¹/₂-inch-diameter dowel, sandpaper, twigs, ¹/₈-inch dowel, ¹/₂-inch red ribbon (optional), paint, varnish.

TOOLS:

Scroll or band saw, drill (lathe, if you want to turn it).

METHOD:

1. Transfer pattern to wood and cut out. (If you turn it on a lathe, set up and turn as you would any pattern).
2. Locate and drill holes for arms (twigs) and nose (¹/₈-inch dowel). Glue nose in place, extending out ¹/₈ inch or so.
3. Prime all surfaces and apply white paint.
4. Sketch all details with soft pencil.
5. Paint eyes, nose, buttons black.
6. The ribbon may be painted red, or simply attach a ¹/₂-inch red ribbon and tie into bow.
7. Paint hatband red.
8. Glue twigs in place for arms.
9. Apply top coat of varnish.

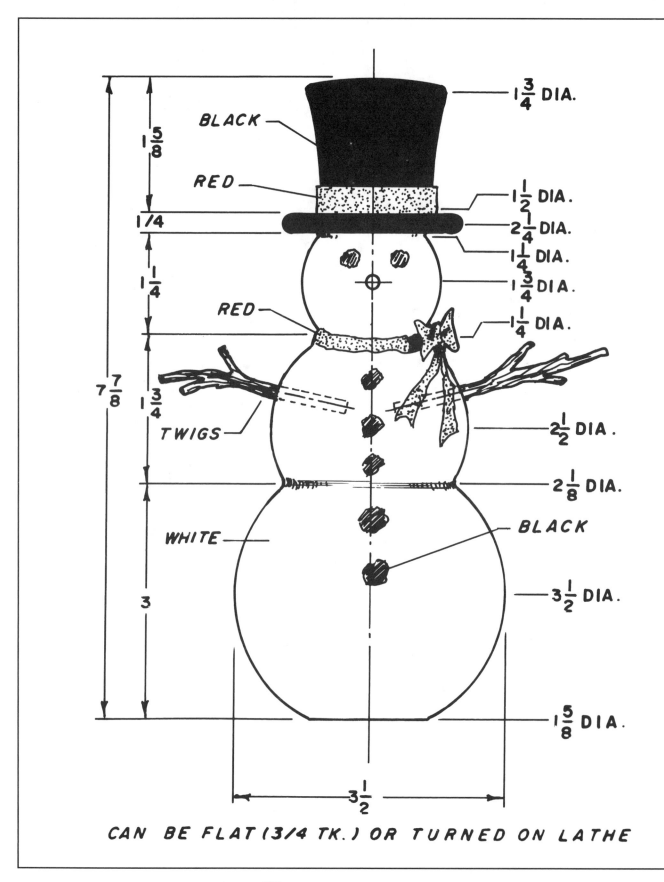

BLACK

RED

$1\frac{3}{4}$ DIA.

$1\frac{1}{2}$ DIA.

$2\frac{1}{4}$ DIA.

$1\frac{1}{4}$ DIA.

$1\frac{3}{4}$ DIA.

$1\frac{1}{4}$ DIA.

$1\frac{5}{8}$

1/4

$1\frac{1}{4}$

$7\frac{7}{8}$

$1\frac{3}{4}$

RED

TWIGS

WHITE

BLACK

$2\frac{1}{2}$ DIA.

$2\frac{1}{8}$ DIA.

3

$3\frac{1}{2}$ DIA.

$1\frac{5}{8}$ DIA.

$3\frac{1}{2}$

CAN BE FLAT (3/4 TK.) OR TURNED ON LATHE

St. Nick's Sled

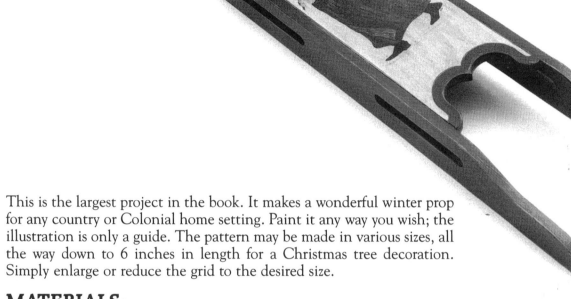

This is the largest project in the book. It makes a wonderful winter prop for any country or Colonial home setting. Paint it any way you wish; the illustration is only a guide. The pattern may be made in various sizes, all the way down to 6 inches in length for a Christmas tree decoration. Simply enlarge or reduce the grid to the desired size.

MATERIALS:
(As drawn) 3/4-inch wood, finishing nails, sandpaper, glue, primer, paint, varnish.

TOOLS:
Band saw, saber saw, drill, hammer.

METHOD:
1. Transfer patterns to wood and cut all parts exactly, using bill of materials list.
2. Temporarily tack runners together.
3. On the top piece, lightly draw 1-inch grid at both ends and lay out pattern of runners.
4. Locate and drill four 3/4-inch holes at beginning and end of each slot, 8 inches apart. Cut out 2 slots with saber saw; sand.
5. Cut front and back shapes; sand.
6. Separate runners.
7. Lay out and cut top board using given 4-inch radius (front) and 1-inch grid (back).
8. Glue and nail pieces together, keeping everything square. Sand all surfaces.
9. Prime all surfaces.
10. Paint sled an old forest green, with an antique white center.
11. Outline white center with thin red stripe.
12. Choose a design and enlarge to fit onto sled.
13. Apply top coat of clear satin varnish.

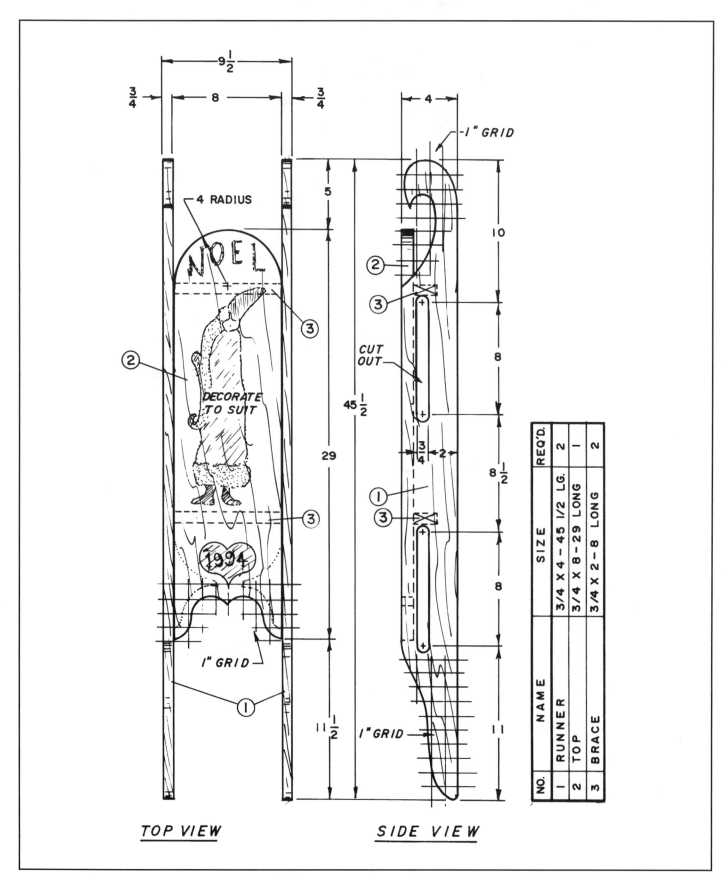

TOP VIEW

SIDE VIEW

NO.	NAME	SIZE	REQ'D.
1	RUNNER	3/4 X 4 – 45 1/2 LG.	2
2	TOP	3/4 X 8 – 29 LONG	1
3	BRACE	3/4 X 2 – 8 LONG	2

Santa in Sleigh with Packages

My grandchildren, Hilary and Daniel, really love this project. Both have a Santa and reindeer to decorate their rooms.

MATERIALS:

⅛-inch plywood, ½-inch scrap wood, ⅛-inch and ³/₁₆-inch dowels, tacks, glue, colorful string or twine, artist acrylic paint, metallic brass paint, varnish, small eyescrews.

TOOLS:

Scroll saw, drill, clamps.

METHOD:

1. Lay out a full-size pattern using 1-inch grid.
2. Transfer pattern to wood and cut all pieces.
3. Locate and drill holes.
4. Assemble sleigh with glue and temporarily add pull sticks and reindeer.
5. Prime all pieces.
6. Paint sleigh burgundy red. Draw a wreath. With small round brush, pick up a little green and a touch of brown. Paint wreath with dabbing motion. Paint ribbon golden brown with antique white for shading.
7. Paint runners with quick-drying metallic brass.
8. Paint poles that attach reindeer to sleigh with metallic brass.
9. Paint Santa suit red with white trim; gloves and boots are black. Outline eyes with black.
10. Paint reindeer burnt umber mixed with white. Paint tails and stomachs white. Paint hooves and antlers white with burnt umber highlights. Halters and harness are black.
11. Cut scrap pieces of wood into squares and rectangular shapes; paint each so they look like wrapped gifts. Make different sizes, shapes, and colors.
12. Attach pull rods to reindeer.
13. Add small eyescrews to reindeer and thread string or twine back to hands.
14. Finish with coat of varnish.
15. Fill sleigh with gifts and trimmings.

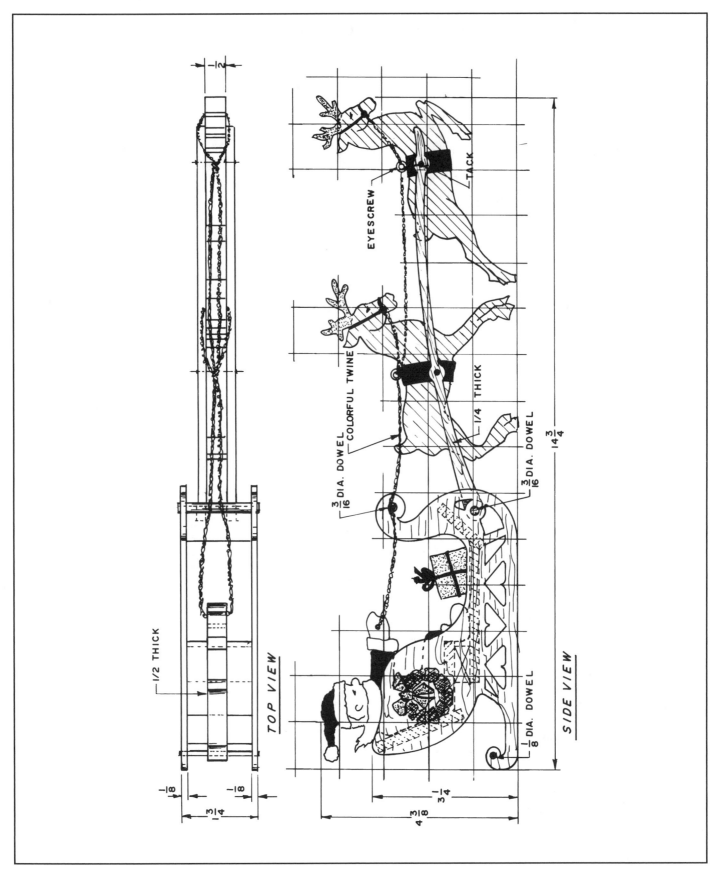

1/2"

TOP VIEW

$\frac{1}{8}$

$\frac{1}{8}$

$\frac{3}{4}$

EYESCREW

TACK

COLORFUL TWINE

$\frac{3}{16}$ DIA. DOWEL

1/4" THICK

$\frac{3}{16}$ DIA. DOWEL

$\frac{1}{8}$ DIA. DOWEL

SIDE VIEW

$14\frac{3}{4}$

$3\frac{1}{4}$

$4\frac{3}{8}$

Tree Trivet

Here's the perfect trivet to use during your holiday entertaining. It's beautiful even if you use it just as a decoration.

MATERIALS:
1/2-inch wood, primer, paint, varnish.

TOOLS:
Scroll saw, drill.

METHOD:
1. Prime wood.
2. Transfer pattern to wood.
3. Paint tree and decorations before cutting out.
4. Drill holes where each cutout will be made (22 holes).
5. Make all inside cuts.
6. Cut out outer edge.
7. Apply clear satin varnish.

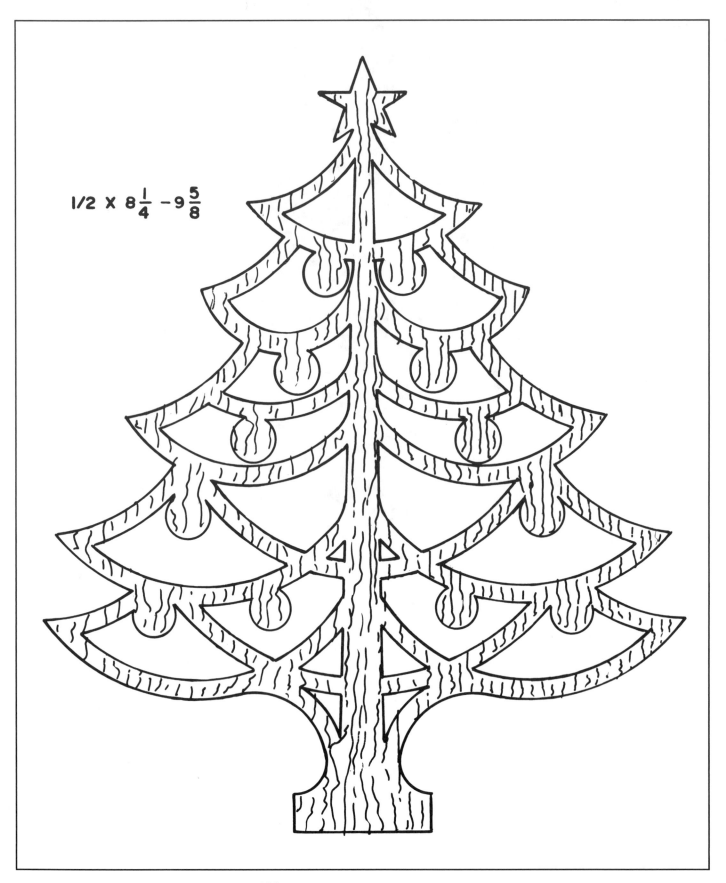

$$1/2 \times 8\frac{1}{4} - 9\frac{5}{8}$$

Pineapple

This festive project will add warmth to your holidays, since the pineapple was a sign of hospitality in early America. It can be made any size; the one pictured is 11 by 13$^7/_8$ inches.

MATERIALS:

Pine or plywood, primer, acrylic latex enamel brown paint, vellum to cut for stencil, stencil brush, masking tape, spray paint (antique bronze), luster gold enamel, dark-green paint, light-green paint, acrylic satin varnish.

TOOLS:

Saber or scroll saw, $^1/_4$-inch drill, sandpaper, X-acto knife.

METHOD:

1. Transfer pattern to wood.
2. Cut out pineapple with saw; drill the $^1/_4$-inch hole.
3. Sand all sides lightly.
4. To finish as illustrated, prime all surfaces.
5. When dry, sand lightly and apply brown paint to all sides.
6. Make a full-size photocopy of pineapple pattern on vellum or heavy plastic for stenciling.
7. Cut out design with X-acto knife.
8. Position and tape stencil to wood. Mask off leaves with scrap paper.
9. Spray body of pineapple with antique bronze paint.
10. To give "body" or "depth," add a coat of luster gold enamel with stencil brush. Try to get a shading effect by dabbing gold to one side of each opening of stencil pattern.
11. Unmask leaves and stencil them with dark-green paint.
12. Dab lighter green along edges of leaves to create "depth."
13. For even more shading or highlighting on leaves, apply antique gold paint along one edge of each. The secret of stenciling is sparse use of paint.
14. When dry, add a few coats of satin varnish.

$\frac{1}{4}$ DIA. HOLE

SIZE:
$\frac{3}{4}$ X 11− 13$\frac{7}{8}$

1″ GRID

FRONT VIEW

110

Noel and
Stained-Glass Noel

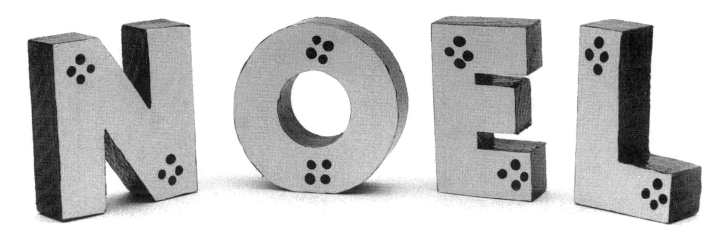

The first of these pretty Noels is cut from ³/₄-inch wood; the other pattern is for an optional stained-glass Noel.

MATERIALS:
³/₄-inch wood, primer, artist acrylic paint, rubber cement, varnish.

TOOLS:
Scroll saw, drill.

METHOD:
1. Copy pattern and cement it to wood.
2. Carefully cut out all letters.
3. Prime all surfaces.
4. Paint front and back (optional) antique white.
5. Paint edges maroon red; apply top coat of varnish.

Note: You can purchase supplies necessary to make a stained glass Noel using the second pattern.

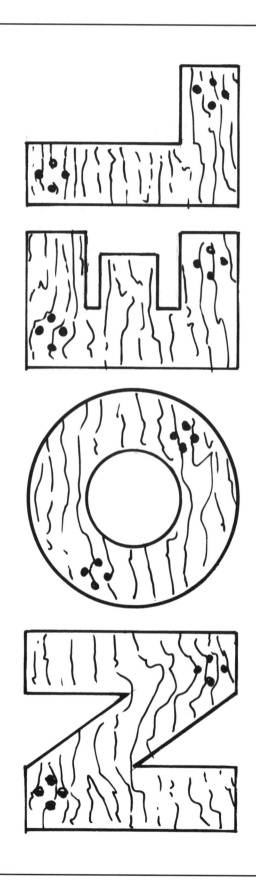

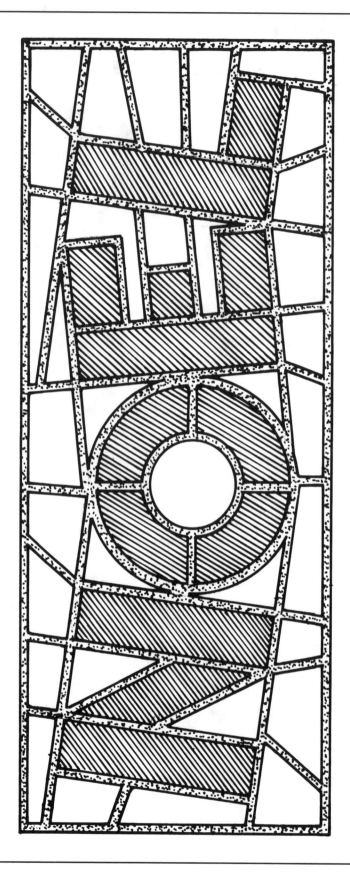

Noel and Joy Candle Holders

These projects add a warm glow to your table when the candles are lighted. Children and grandchildren love them.

MATERIALS:
3/4-inch wood, rubber cement, primer, paint, varnish, 3/8-inch-diameter candles.

TOOLS:
Scroll saw, drill.

METHOD:
1. Copy patterns and cement them to wood.
2. Cut out; sand all edges.
3. Drill holes for candles.
4. These can be left natural with just a top coat of varnish or painted as desired. I simply applied a clear satin varnish to the Noel; for the Joy, I painted the front and back green and the edges red, then applied clear varnish.

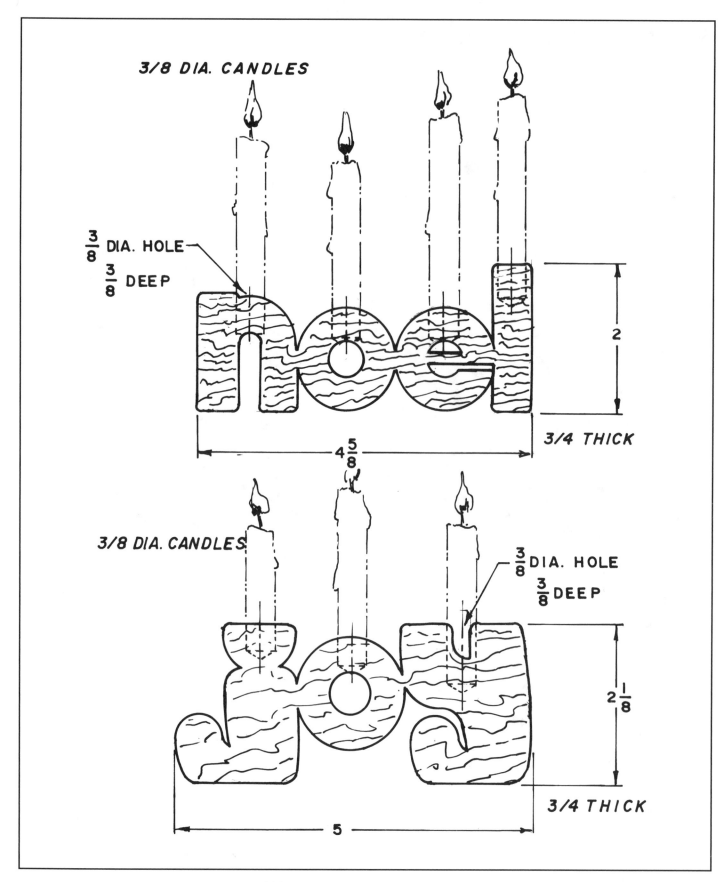

3/8 DIA. CANDLES

$\frac{3}{8}$ DIA. HOLE
$\frac{3}{8}$ DEEP

2

3/4 THICK

$4\frac{5}{8}$

3/8 DIA. CANDLES

$\frac{3}{8}$ DIA. HOLE
$\frac{3}{8}$ DEEP

$2\frac{1}{8}$

3/4 THICK

5

Angel Candle Holder

I have made many copies of this project, since everyone I know who has seen it wanted one! It is as easy to make 2 or 3 as it is to make 1. Give them as Christmas presents.

MATERIALS:
3/8-inch scrap wood, paint, liner brush, varnish, candle holder, candle.

TOOLS:
Scroll saw, drill.

METHOD:
1. Make a full-size copy of pattern and transfer to wood.
2. Cut out all parts and sand.
3. Drill hole in base for candle holder.
4. Glue pieces together.
5. Paint angels antique white and outline robes and wings with liner brush using thinned burnt umber.
6. Hair is golden brown and yellow, with long strokes to simulate strands.
7. Paint base deep river green.
8. When dry, finish with clear satin varnish.
9. Add candle.

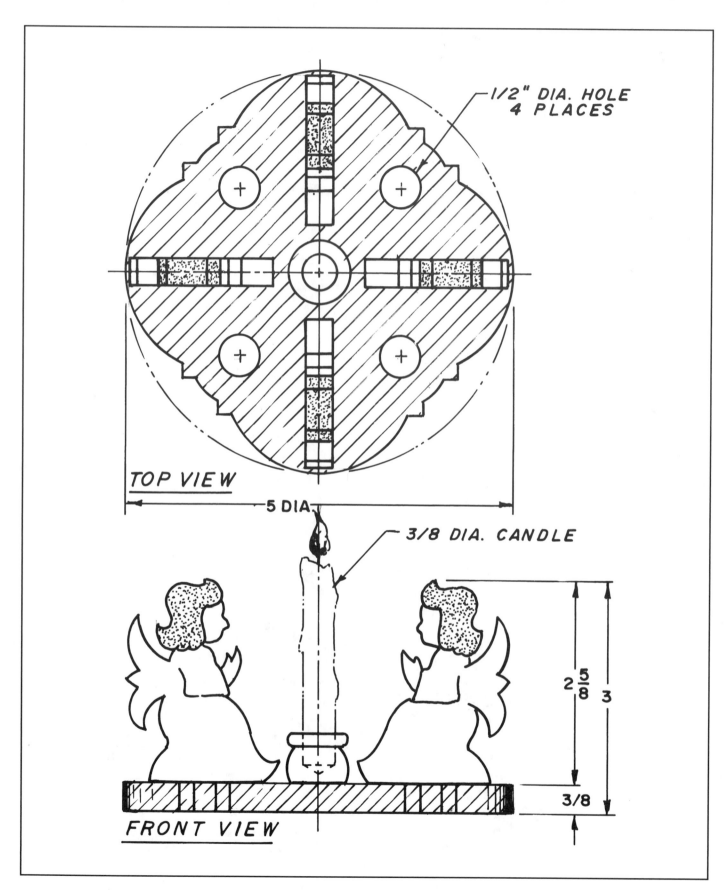

1/2" DIA. HOLE
4 PLACES

TOP VIEW

5 DIA

3/8 DIA. CANDLE

$2\frac{5}{8}$

3

3/8

FRONT VIEW

116

Gingerbread Man Ornament

No Christmas would be complete without this ornament, even if it's made of wood. It will save you from baking gingerbread men every year!

MATERIALS:

3/8-inch to 1/2-inch wood, paint, varnish, string or twine.

TOOLS:

Scroll saw, drill.

METHOD:

1. Transfer pattern to wood and cut out.
2. Paint all surfaces with burnt umber and golden brown mixed. This should look like gingerbread.
3. Draw eyes, nose, mouth, and buttons with pencil and paint black.
4. Apply light top coat of clear satin varnish.

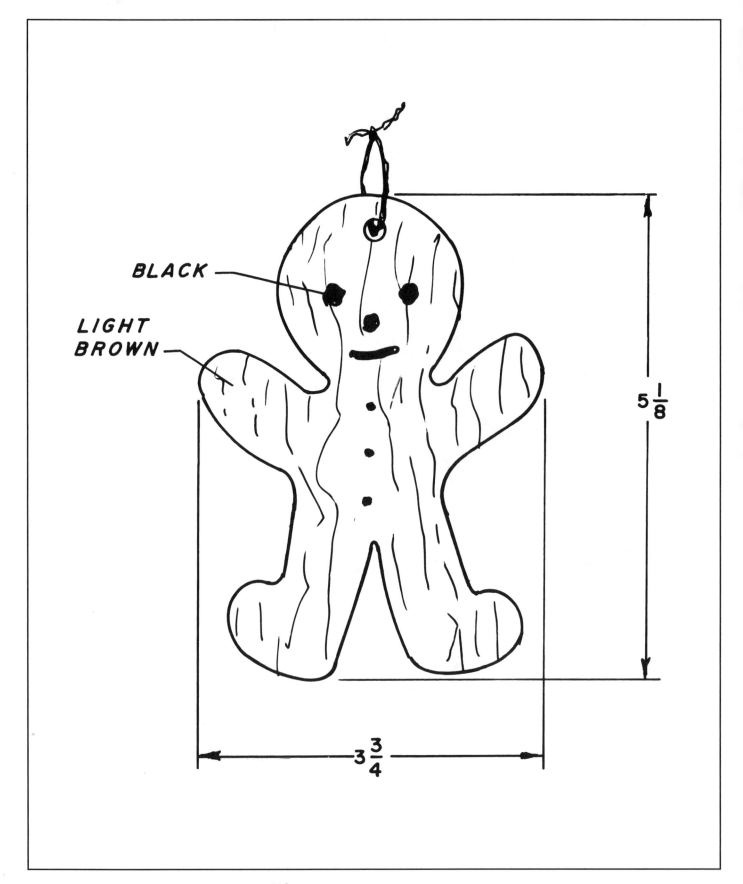

BLACK

LIGHT
BROWN

$5\frac{1}{8}$

$3\frac{3}{4}$

Dove, Angel, Holly, Reindeer, Candy Cane, Snowman

These scroll saw patterns can be used many ways—as Christmas tree ornaments, window shade pulls, or window decorations.

MATERIALS:
1/8-inch to 3/16-inch high-grade plywood, paint, string or twine, rubber cement.

TOOLS:
Scroll saw, drill.

METHOD:
1. Copy each pattern and cement to wood.
2. Drill small starter holes for all interior cuts.
3. Make interior cuts.
4. Cut out outside outline.

5. Leave paper copy in place and paint on top of it, unless you want to leave ornament its natural color.

6. Dove: This may be left its natural color; apply coat of varnish.

7. Angel: Paint with a fast-drying gold enamel. Finish with clear satin varnish.

8. Holly: Prime and paint with artist acrylic deep river green. Mix white and green to get a lighter shade and paint one side. Outline middle and outside of leaves with white. For berries, use wooden end of brush; dab on small amounts of maroon. While this is drying, pick up white paint with end of brush and dab a tiny spot near top of berry. When dry, finish with clear satin varnish.

9. Reindeer: Leave a natural color except for bells, which are painted in quick-drying metallic chrome enamel. Paint both sides. Finish with artist acrylic gloss varnish.

10. Candy cane: Outside is painted ivory. Cane is white with red for thick stripes and yellow for thin stripes. Holly leaves are deep river green with middle and edge white. Mix white with green for lighter shade for shading leaves; shade leaves before painting middles and edges white. Berries are maroon with dab of white for shading (see instructions for holly ornament). Mix maroon and ivory for ribbon. Use maroon for shading ribbon. When dry, apply clear satin varnish.

11. Snowman: Paint outside with artist acrylic ivory. Snowman is ivory with black dots for eyes, black circle for nose, black dots for mouth, and big black dots for buttons. Paint candy cane white with red stripes. Trim cane in black with liner brush. Hat is black with maroon band. Holly is Christmas green with ivory veins and trim on outside. Berries are maroon with white dot near top. Finish with artist acrylic gloss varnish.

Rocking Horse Ornament

Here is a great way to turn small scraps into nice decorations for your tree.

MATERIALS:
3/16-inch scraps, 3/32-inch dowel, artist acrylic paint, clear satin varnish.

TOOLS:
Scroll saw, drill.

METHOD:
1. Copy full-size pattern of head, seat, rocker, and brace.
2. Transfer patterns to wood and cut out.
3. Glue together.
4. Paint the neck, face, and seat white.
5. Back, sides of seat and dowels near face are Christmas green.
6. Bottom section and rocker parts are maroon.
7. Hole for eye is black.
8. Finish with clear satin varnish.
9. Use green yarn to hang ornament.

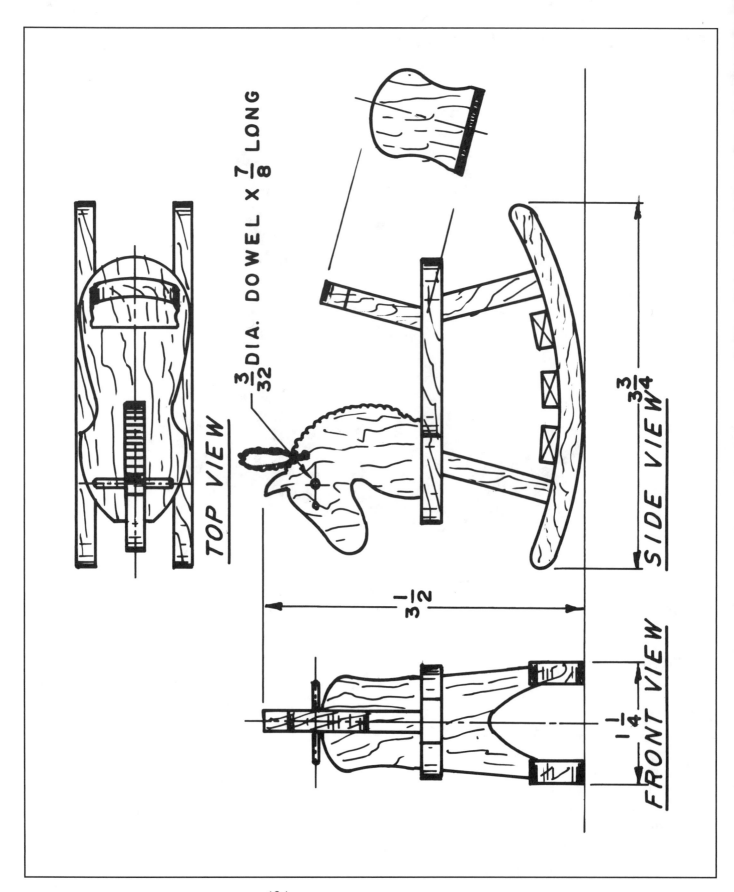

TOP VIEW

$\frac{3}{32}$ DIA. DOWEL X $\frac{7}{8}$ LONG

SIDE VIEW

$3\frac{3}{4}$

$3\frac{1}{2}$

$1\frac{1}{4}$

FRONT VIEW

Santa Ornament

Children will love to make Santa dance—just pull the string and watch his arms and legs move. This project may take a little fitting and filing to make Santa move just right.

MATERIALS:

¼-inch scrap wood, twine, ½-inch wooden ball, ¾-inch brads, artist acrylic paint, quick-drying metallic chrome enamel, clear satin varnish.

TOOLS:

Scroll saw, drill, hammer.

METHOD:

1. Make a full-size copy of page with parts.
2. Rubber cement copy to scraps of wood and carefully cut out; sand lightly.
3. Drill ¹⁄₃₂-inch-diameter holes. Don't forget pull-string holes on edge of arms and legs.
4. From back side of back piece, drive in 4 brads.
5. Turn over and glue center piece to back.
6. Sand arms, legs so they are slightly thinner than ¼ inch.
7. Fit arms and legs to make sure they move correctly. Adjust if necessary.
8. Temporarily add front; recheck that everything still moves properly with front part in place.
9. Take figure apart for painting. Note the 5 sections. Back and center are painted red on sides, except for face and hat.
10. On front section, paint front and sides of suit red.
11. After red is dry, draw details onto face and body on front section. Paint face a flesh color; for cheeks, lips, add a dab of red to paint. Outline eyes in black; paint eyes white with black dot in center.
12. Fur on hat, coat, legs, arms, whiskers, eyebrows are ivory, painted with dabbing motion. Belt, mittens, boots are black.
13. Buckle and bell are metallic chrome. Paint the paper that Santa is holding white, then add "Merry Xmas" in black.
14. Finish with clear satin varnish.
15. See drawing to hook up strings. Paint ball red; when dry, varnish.
16. Reassemble and check that everything moves properly.

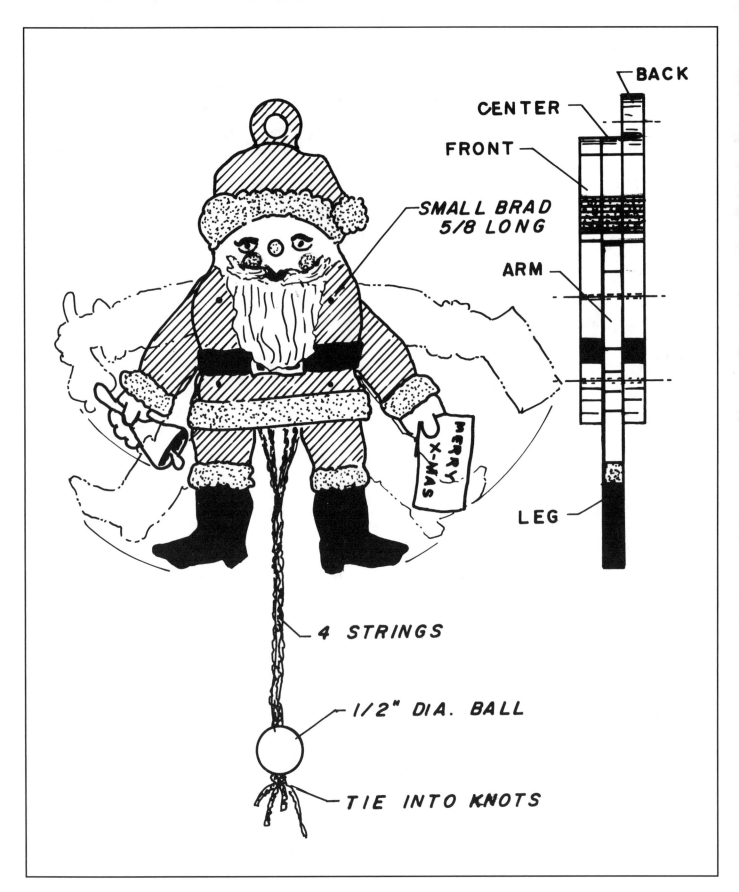

BACK

CENTER

FRONT

SMALL BRAD
5/8 LONG

ARM

LEG

MERRY
X-MAS

4 STRINGS

1/2" DIA. BALL

TIE INTO KNOTS

BACK

$\frac{1}{32}$ DIA. HOLES
(FOR BRADS)

CENTER

$\frac{1}{32}$ DIA. HOLES
(FOR STRING)

RIGHT ARM

LEFT ARM

FRONT

LEGS

Standing Christmas Tree

This simple Christmas tree may be made in various sizes by enlarging the pattern. If you enlarge the pattern, keep the notches the same thickness as the wood you use. This is a handsome centerpiece when little wrapped packages are placed around it.

MATERIALS:
(As illustrated) ¼-inch plywood, primer, artist acrylic paint, hobby craft metallic chrome paint, glue, varnish.

TOOLS:
Scroll saw.

METHOD:
1. Make two copies of pattern and transfer them to wood.
2. Cut out each pattern; make one notch from bottom as shown and one notch from top so pieces can slide together.
3. Slide pieces together and glue. Bottoms must line up.
4. Prime and paint deep river green.
5. Using No. 6 round brush, shade tree with blue spruce paint using long and short sweeping strokes.
6. Paint trunk light brown with dark brown for shading.
7. Paint stand maroon.
8. Draw ornaments on tree.
9. Paint star metallic chrome and ornaments various colors.
10. When dry, finish with clear satin varnish.

128

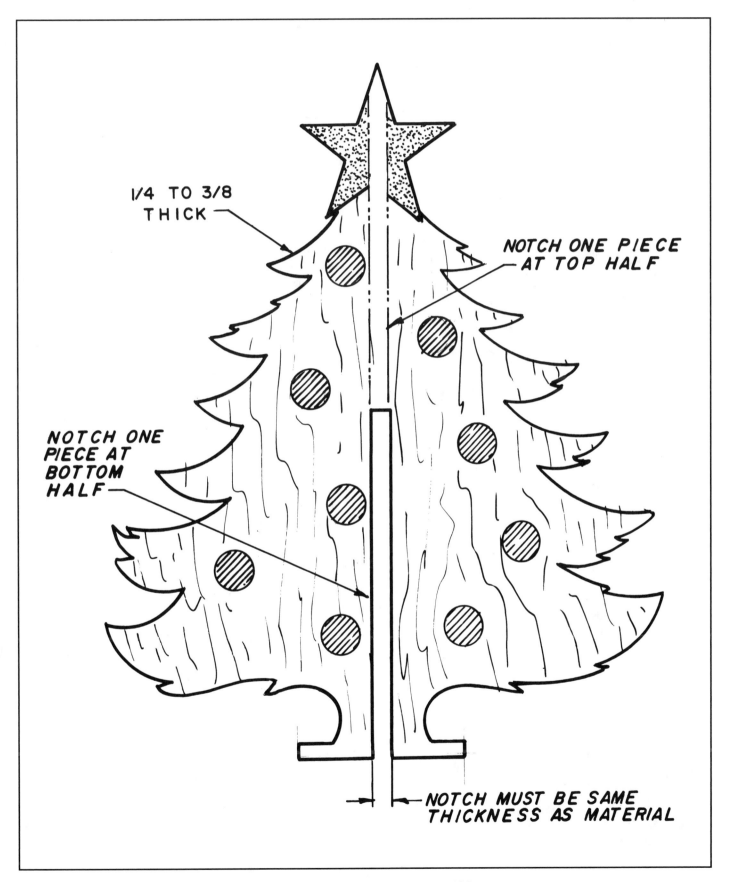

1/4 TO 3/8 THICK

NOTCH ONE PIECE AT TOP HALF

NOTCH ONE PIECE AT BOTTOM HALF

NOTCH MUST BE SAME THICKNESS AS MATERIAL

Santa Face on a Stick

This originated with a large 3-foot plastic Santa face I saw in a department store.

MATERIALS:

1/2-inch and 3/4-inch wood, 1/4-inch dowel, primer, artist acrylic paint, liner brush, varnish.

TOOLS:

Scroll saw, drill, router (optional).

METHOD:

1. Copy pattern and transfer to wood.
2. Cut out; sand lightly.
3. Locate and drill a 1/4-inch-diameter hole in from edge about an inch or so.
4. Cut a 1/4-inch dowel off at 5 5/8 inches.
5. Make up base about 2 by 3 1/2 inches. Drill 1/4-inch-diameter hole in center. (Optional: With router, make a 1/8-inch-radius cove cut as shown.)
6. Prime all surfaces.
7. With soft pencil, sketch all details as illustrated on both sides.
8. Paint stand red, pole green.
9. Paint face a skin color and add red cheeks.
10. Paint eyebrows, mustache, and beard white with long, sweeping strokes.
11. Paint lips pink.
12. Paint hat red, trim white. Use dabbing motion on trim; this will create a fur look.
13. Outline entire face with black paint and liner brush.
14. Finish with top coat of clear satin varnish.

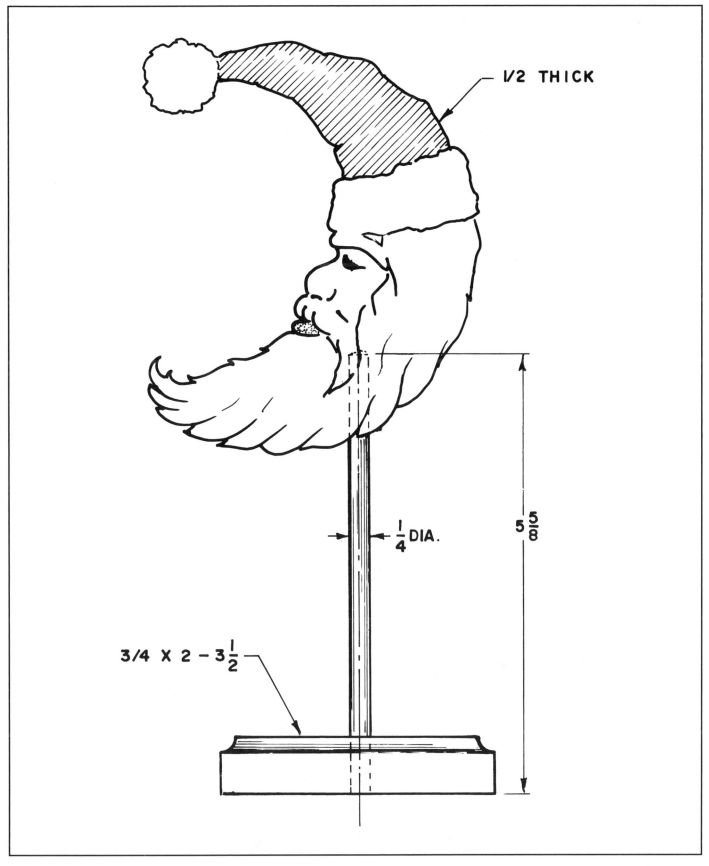

1/2 THICK

$\frac{1}{4}$ DIA.

$5\frac{5}{8}$

3/4 X 2 − $3\frac{1}{2}$

131

Folk Art Santa

Here's a whimsical decoration that's bound to get noticed.

MATERIALS:
1/2-inch and 3/4-inch wood, 1/4-inch dowel, primer, artist acrylic paint, liner brush, metallic brass enamel paint, varnish.

TOOLS:
Scroll saw, drill, router (optional).

METHOD:
1. Copy pattern and transfer to wood.
2. Cut out; sand lightly.
3. Locate and drill a 1/4-inch-diameter hole in from edge about an inch or so.
4. Cut a 1/4-inch dowel off at 5 5/8 inches.
5. Make base about 2 by 3 1/2 inches. Drill a 1/4-inch hole in center. (Optional: With router, make a 1/8-inch-radius cove cut.)
6. Prime all surfaces.
7. With soft pencil, sketch all details as illustrated on both sides.
8. Paint stand red and pole green.
9. Paint face a skin color and add red cheeks.
10. Paint beard, eyebrows white, using dabbing motion to give look of hair.
11. Eyes are outlined in black.
12. Horn is painted with quick-drying metallic brass.
13. Hat, suit are red with white trim. Paint trim with dabbing motion.
14. Boot, mitten, belt are black. Bag is green.
15. Finish by outlining everything in black with liner brush. When dry, finish with clear satin varnish.

Christmas Canada Goose

This makes a beautiful centerpiece to be filled or decorated with greens or pinecones.

MATERIALS:

3/8-inch and 1/2-inch wood, finishing nails, glue, primer, paint, walnut stain, varnish.

TOOLS:

Band saw, table saw, hammer.

METHOD:

1. Make a full-size pattern of head using 1/2-inch grid and transfer to 1/2-inch wood.
2. Cut out; sand.
3. Cut sides and bottom of bowl out of 3/8-inch wood. Note ends are cut at 45 degrees. Bowl may be any length or width; mine was slightly less than the 13-inch overall length shown.
4. Glue and nail bowl pieces together.
5. Sand all surfaces.
6. Glue and nail head in place, centered on inside-front end as shown.
7. Prime. When dry, use pattern in book to draw pattern onto goose.
8. Body is grayish black with some white on it, black beak, and black eye. Refer to the drawing.
9. When dry, apply walnut stain over all surfaces; wipe off excess immediately. This will give an antique look.
10. When dry, finish with clear satin varnish.

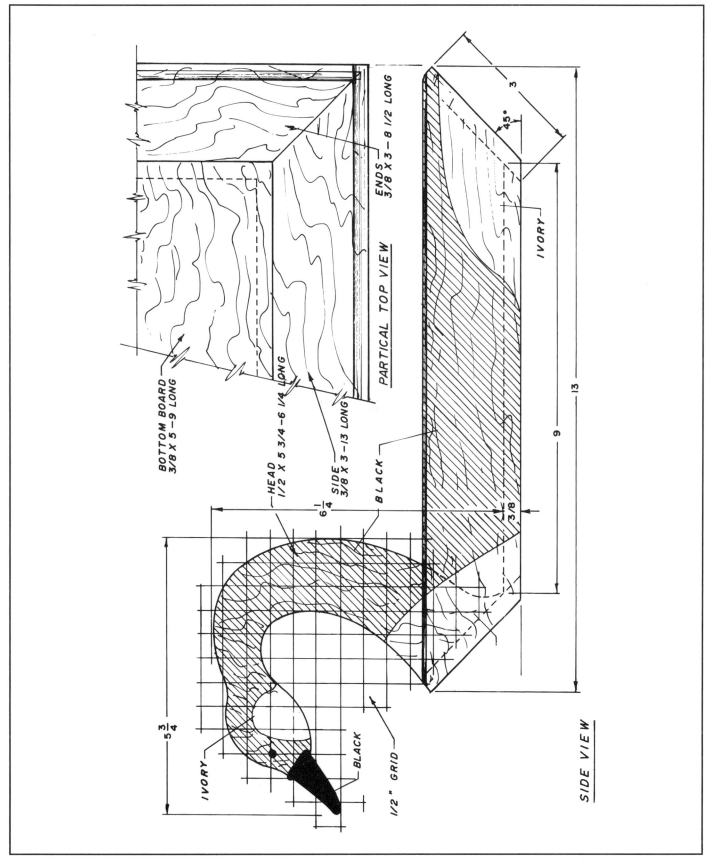

PARTICAL TOP VIEW

ENDS
3/8 X 3 — 8 1/2 LONG

IVORY

BOTTOM BOARD
3/8 X 5 — 9 LONG

HEAD
1/2 X 5 3/4 — 6 1/4 LONG

SIDE
3/8 X 3 — 13 LONG

BLACK

3

45°

13

9

3/8

6 1/4

5 3/4

IVORY

BLACK

1/2" GRID

SIDE VIEW

Santa Standing by a Tree

This decoration finds Santa in his native element!

MATERIALS:
3/8-inch wood, glue, artist acrylic paint, clear satin varnish.

TOOLS:
Scroll saw.

METHOD:
1. Using a 1/2-inch grid, lay out pattern. Base (or shelf) is simply a 2 3/4-inch radius.
2. Cut out all pieces; sand lightly.
3. Glue tree and base together. Use rubber bands to hold pieces until glue sets. Note base is positioned up about 3/4 inch from bottom surface.
4. Paint tree back, front, and sides with Christmas green. Stand that Santa stands on is dark green; bottom is brown.
5. Sponge paint tree dark green with upward strokes. Start at bottom and work up. Include sides and back. This will give shading and a look of branches with needles.
6. With small paintbrush, dab on ivory to look like snow. Refer to drawing.
7. Apply clear satin varnish.
8. Transfer pattern of Santa to wood freehand or with tracing paper. You must transfer both sides.
9. Face is skin color; eyes are black; eyebrows, mustache, beard are ivory. Cheeks, nose tip, cap are red iron oxide. Trim on cap, face edge, and pom-pom are ivory. Coat is red iron oxide with ivory cuffs and trim. Use dabbing motion on fur, hat trim, and beard. Mittens and boots are black. Tree Santa is holding is painted Christmas green with dab of brown to give some shading. Tree trunk is brown. When dry, paint on snow as you did above.
10. Finish with clear satin varnish.

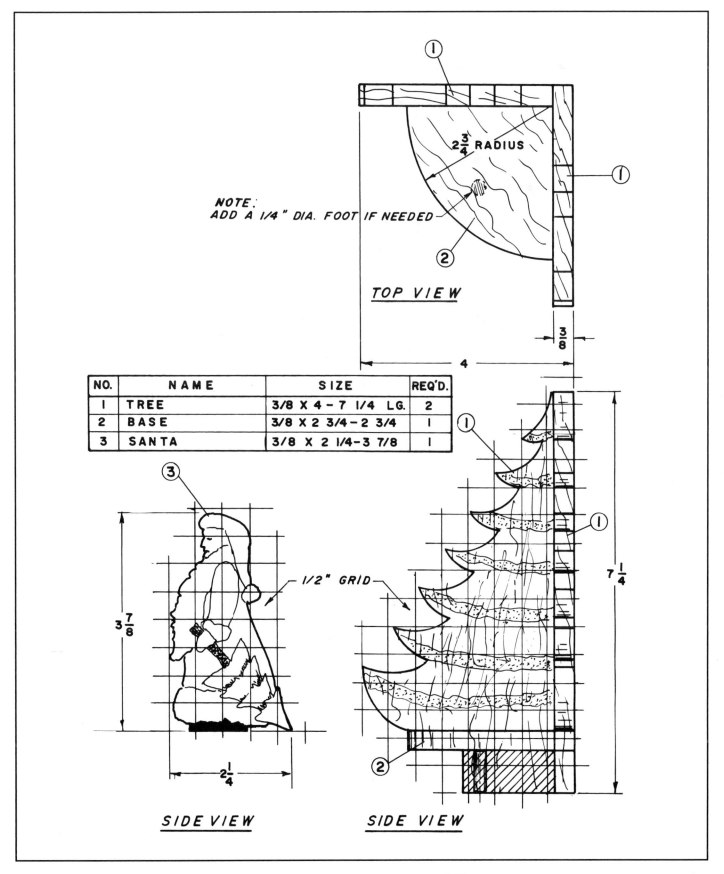

① TREE

NOTE:
ADD A 1/4" DIA. FOOT IF NEEDED

$2\frac{3}{4}$ RADIUS

② BASE

TOP VIEW

$\frac{3}{8}$

4

NO.	NAME	SIZE	REQ'D.
1	TREE	3/8 X 4 – 7 1/4 LG.	2
2	BASE	3/8 X 2 3/4 – 2 3/4	1
3	SANTA	3/8 X 2 1/4 – 3 7/8	1

③

$7\frac{1}{4}$

$3\frac{7}{8}$

1/2" GRID

$2\frac{1}{4}$

②

SIDE VIEW   *SIDE VIEW*

137

Christmas Scoop
(for Napkins, Cards)

This small scoop may be used for many things—to hold little holiday napkins or your Christmas cards, as you receive them.

MATERIALS:
¼-inch wood, glue, sandpaper, primer, artist acrylic paint, varnish.

TOOLS:
Saw, drill.

METHOD:
1. Cut all pieces to overall sizes; sand all surfaces.
2. Cut the 2 sides and sand.
3. Lay out and cut handle of back piece. Tip is cut at 10 degrees.
4. Assemble with glue. Use rubber band to hold pieces while glue sets.
5. Prime all surfaces.
6. Paint burgundy rose.
7. I decided this was too plain, so I added holly leaves. Find a pattern with holly leaves and draw them on freehand or trace pattern. Paint edges of leaves white, then double-load your brush, with forest green on one side and deep river green on the other. Paint leaves, blending colors to your liking. With liner brush, just barely paint tips of leaves white. Use thinned burnt umber for leaf veins. Berries are painted red with the wooden end of brush; just use a dab for each berry. To highlight, put a tiny dab of white near top of each berry.
8. Finish with clear satin varnish.

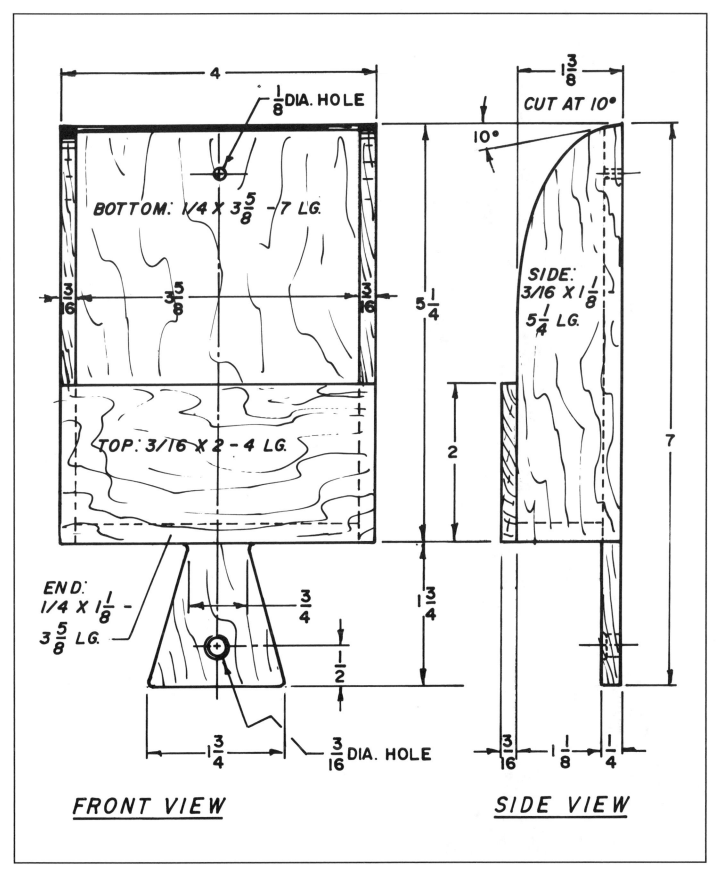

$\frac{1}{8}$ DIA. HOLE

4

BOTTOM: 1/4 X 3$\frac{5}{8}$ - 7 LG.

$\frac{3}{16}$ $\frac{5}{8}$ $\frac{3}{16}$

TOP: 3/16 X 2 - 4 LG.

END:
1/4 X 1$\frac{1}{8}$ -
3$\frac{5}{8}$ LG.

$\frac{3}{4}$

$\frac{1}{2}$

1$\frac{3}{4}$

$\frac{3}{16}$ DIA. HOLE

5$\frac{1}{4}$

2

1$\frac{3}{4}$

FRONT VIEW

1$\frac{3}{8}$

CUT AT 10°

10°

SIDE:
3/16 X 1$\frac{1}{8}$
5$\frac{1}{4}$ LG.

7

$\frac{3}{16}$ 1$\frac{1}{8}$ $\frac{1}{4}$

SIDE VIEW

Toy Soldier

When I think of Christmas, I think of "The March of the Tin Soldiers." Here is my version of a toy soldier.

MATERIALS:

1/4-inch and 1/2-inch wood, 3/16-inch dowel, artist acrylic paint, varnish.

TOOLS:

Scroll saw, drill.

METHOD:

1. Make full-size pattern with 1-inch grid, as given.
2. Transfer pattern to wood and cut out.
3. Drill 3/16-inch holes as noted.
4. Prime all surfaces.
5. Transfer details of soldier onto wood freehand or by tracing.
6. To paint, follow colors marked on drawing.
7. Assemble after painting; make sure arms and legs move. If not, sand a little where arms and legs join body.
8. Finish with clear satin varnish.

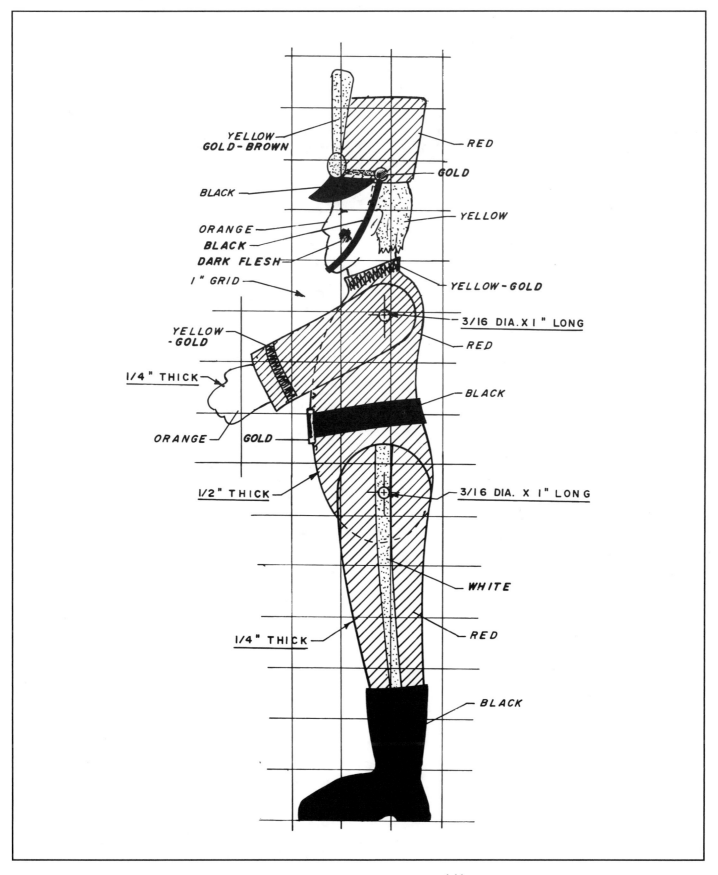

YELLOW
GOLD-BROWN

RED

BLACK

GOLD

ORANGE

YELLOW

BLACK

DARK FLESH

1" GRID

YELLOW-GOLD

YELLOW
-GOLD

3/16 DIA. X 1" LONG

RED

1/4" THICK

BLACK

ORANGE

GOLD

1/2" THICK

3/16 DIA. X 1" LONG

WHITE

RED

1/4" THICK

BLACK

141

Angel on a Stick

I know that this is another project on a stick, but how else do you expect your angel to fly? It will add a lot to the holiday decorations around your house.

MATERIALS:

1/2-inch and 3/4-inch wood, 5/16-inch dowel, artist acrylic paint, quick-drying enamel metallic brass, varnish.

TOOLS:

Scroll saw, drill.

METHOD:

1. Lay out pattern on 1/2-inch grid.
2. Transfer pattern to 1/2-inch wood; cut out.
3. Cut out base from 3/4-inch wood.
4. Drill 5/16-inch holes in base and body.
5. Cut a 5/16-inch dowel 8 inches long.
6. Prime all surfaces.
7. Paint stand burnt umber. When dry, add a wash coat of forest green.
8. Paint stick burnt umber.
9. Paint star with quick-drying brass enamel.
10. Dress is picket white; ribbon, midnight blue; face, arm, a flesh color. Outline eye with black; paint eyeball midnight blue. Hair is straw color; when dry, use straw color again, and use sweeping strokes with brush to give look of hair.
11. Paint wings ivory; when dry, paint again with ivory and golden brown. Pick up ivory with brush and a dab of golden brown; wiping off excess, paint with pouncing or dabbing motion. This gives a feathery look.
12. Apply clear satin varnish.
13. When dry, rub some shoe polish onto dress, wings, hair for shading.
14. Apply top coat of clear satin varnish.

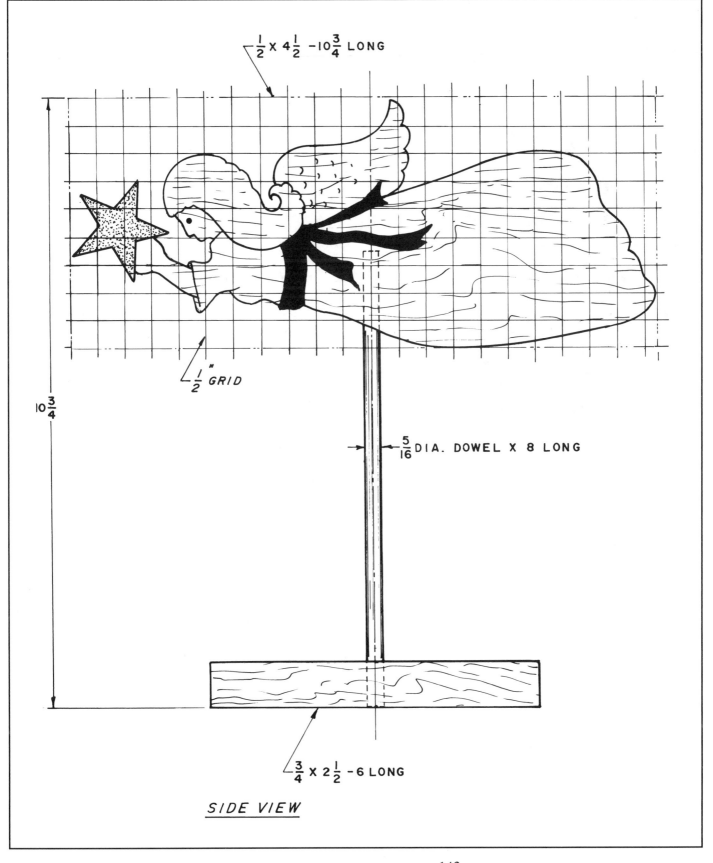

$\frac{1}{2}$ X $4\frac{1}{2}$ –$10\frac{3}{4}$ LONG

$\frac{1}{2}$" GRID

$10\frac{3}{4}$

$\frac{5}{16}$ DIA. DOWEL X 8 LONG

$\frac{3}{4}$ X $2\frac{1}{2}$ –6 LONG

SIDE VIEW

Christmas Tree Puzzle

This makes a wonderful Christmas keepsake for a child.

MATERIALS:

$3/16$-inch or $1/4$-inch high-quality plywood (no voids)—2 sheets $10 1/2$ by $14 1/4$ inches overall size, artist acrylic paint, varnish.

TOOLS:

Scroll saw, drill.

METHOD:

1. Using $1/2$-inch grid, lay out tree and decorations, as shown.
2. Cut and trim sheets of plywood to size above. Sand edges.
3. Prime top of one sheet of plywood; sand lightly.
4. Center and transfer pattern of tree and decorations onto primed wood.
5. Paint tree Christmas green. When dry, sponge paint in forest green, starting at bottom and using short, sweeping motion to shade branches and give appearance of needles.
6. Paint, decorate ornaments as desired. Paint base, "Joy," and star. After painting, outline "Joy" in black.
7. Paint area around tree white.
8. Drill $1/32$-inch hole at corner of a branch. Insert saw blade and cut out tree.
9. Drill $1/32$-inch holes at corner of each ornament and cut out each.
10. Glue top piece of plywood (with tree cut out) to other piece.
11. Paint area of bottom board where tree is cut out yellow. Keep paint off top piece of wood.
12. Paint edges, back of plywood base in red. Do not paint edges of cutout area.
13. When dry, assemble puzzle. Pieces must go together easily; sand edges lightly if fit is too tight.
14. Finish with clear satin varnish.

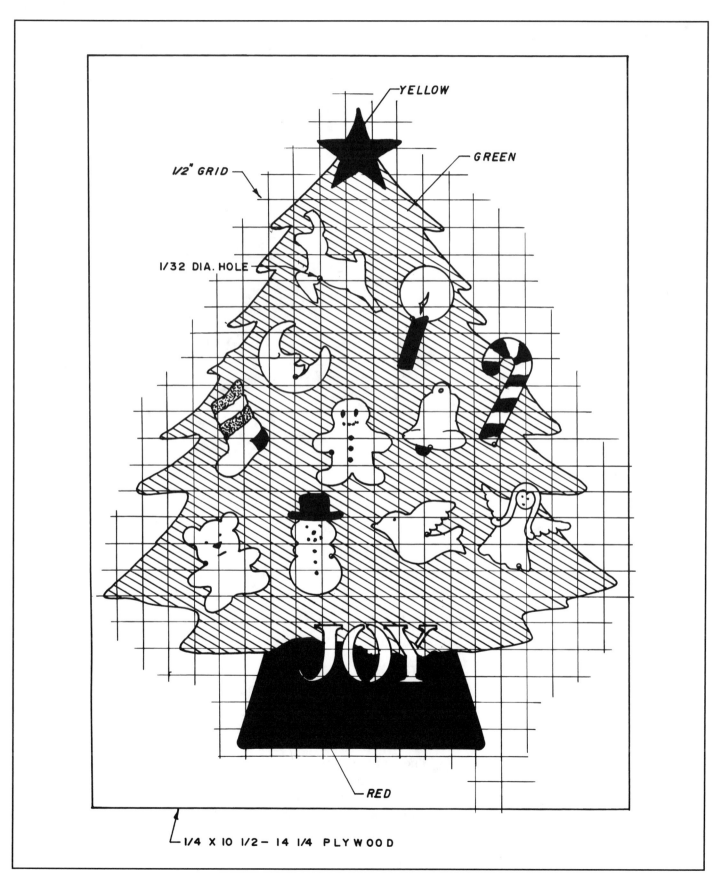

Christmas Tree Candelabra

This project provides light as well as a festive touch to your table or mantle.

MATERIALS:
1/2-inch and 3/4-inch wood, candles, artist acrylic paint, quick-drying metallic brass paint, varnish.

TOOLS:
Scroll saw, drill.

METHOD:
1. Lay out a full-size pattern using a 1-inch grid. (Note: Base is half round, 6 inches wide, 3-inch radius).
2. Transfer shape to wood and cut out.
3. Drill 3/8-inch holes for candles.
4. Glue parts together.
5. Paint with blue spruce, including stand.
6. Repaint stand maroon.
7. Referring to drawing, paint dots on stand in brass. Use wooden end of brush.
8. Finish with clear satin varnish.
9. Add candles.

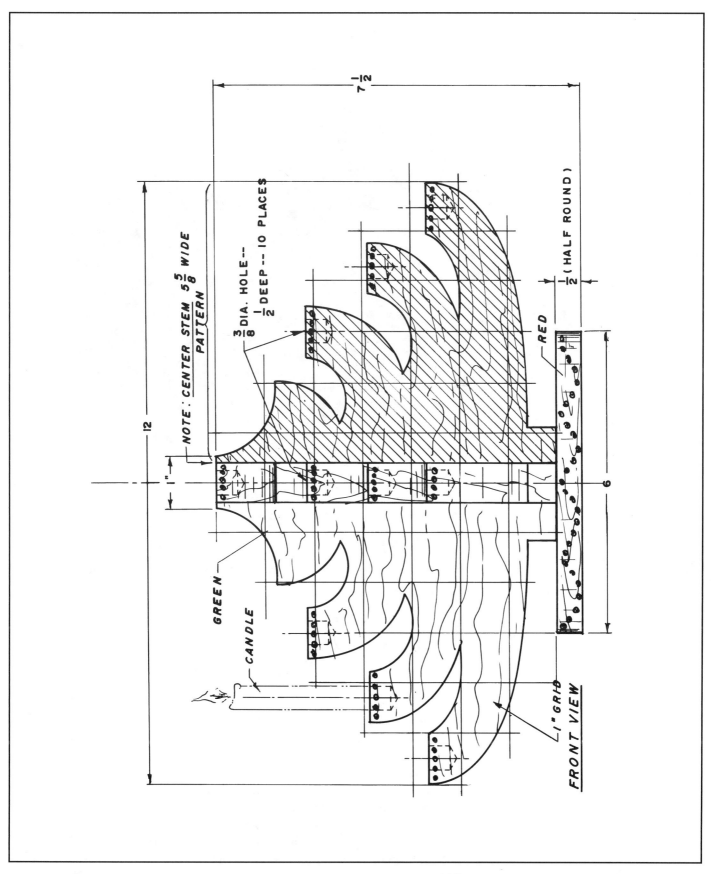

NOTE: CENTER STEM $5\frac{5}{8}$ WIDE PATTERN

$\frac{3}{8}$ DIA. HOLE -- $\frac{1}{2}$ DEEP -- 10 PLACES

$7\frac{1}{2}$

$\frac{1}{2}$ (HALF ROUND)

RED

12

6

1"

GREEN

CANDLE

1" GRID

FRONT VIEW

Crêche

Though it is intricate, this soundly built project will last a lifetime. I've lived on a farm and tried to make it look like a real Nativity scene.

MATERIALS:

¼-inch plywood, ¾-inch scrap wood, brads, glue, stain, varnish.

TOOLS:

Table or hand saw, hammer.

METHOD:

1. Lay out and cut out back piece from plywood. Build rest of crêche around this piece.
2. Cut out roof. Make sure ends are at correct angles. Dry fit all pieces to back board.
3. Cut and fit all other pieces to complete scene. (See next project for crêche figures.)
4. Paint inside of crêche antique white. Outside is gray.
5. When dry, apply walnut stain, then wipe off excess. With cloth, apply stain to roof with a dabbing motion.
6. When dry, apply clear satin varnish to all surfaces.
7. When dry, apply woodworking glue to several areas on crêche floor, then scatter straw. Press down to make straw adhere to glue spots.

148

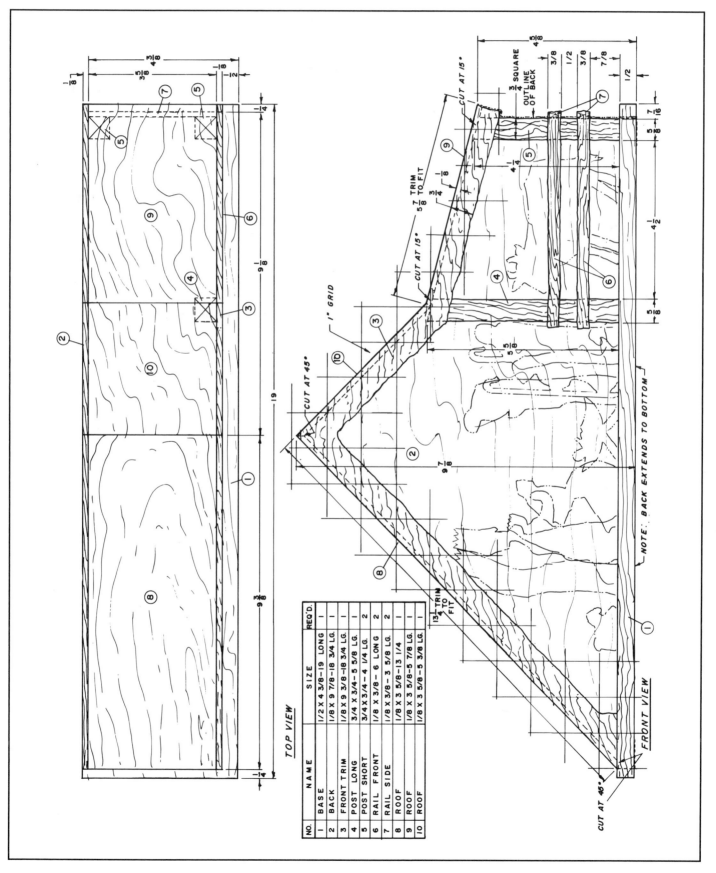

TOP VIEW

FRONT VIEW

1" GRID

CUT AT 45°

CUT AT 15°

CUT AT 15°

NOTE: BACK EXTENDS TO BOTTOM

3/4 SQUARE

OUTLINE OF BACK

TRIM TO FIT

TRIM TO FIT

NO.	NAME	SIZE	REQ'D.
1	BASE	1/2 X 4 3/8 – 19 LONG	1
2	BACK	1/8 x 9 7/8 –18 3/4 LG.	1
3	FRONT TRIM	1/8 X 9 3/8 –18 3/4 LG.	1
4	POST LONG	3/4 X 3/4 – 5 5/8 LG.	1
5	POST SHORT	3/4 X 3/4 – 4 1/4 LG.	2
6	RAIL FRONT	1/8 X 3/8 – 6 LONG	2
7	RAIL SIDE	1/8 X 3/8 – 3 5/8 LG.	2
8	ROOF	1/8 X 3 5/8 –13 1/4	1
9	ROOF	1/8 X 3 5/8 – 5 7/8 LG.	1
10	ROOF	1/8 X 3 5/8 – 5 3/8 LG.	1

Crêche Figures

This is the fun part—making the figures for the scene. They may be stained and left plain, as I did, or painted and detailed as you desire. Look for crêches in books and magazines for ideas.

MATERIALS:

3/4-inch scraps, paint, clear satin varnish.

TOOLS:

Scroll saw.

METHOD:

1. Transfer patterns to wood.
2. Cut out each; sand lightly.
3. Paint edges of figures brown.
4. When dry, sand any paint off front or back of figures.
5. Finish with 2 coats of clear satin varnish, sanding between coats.

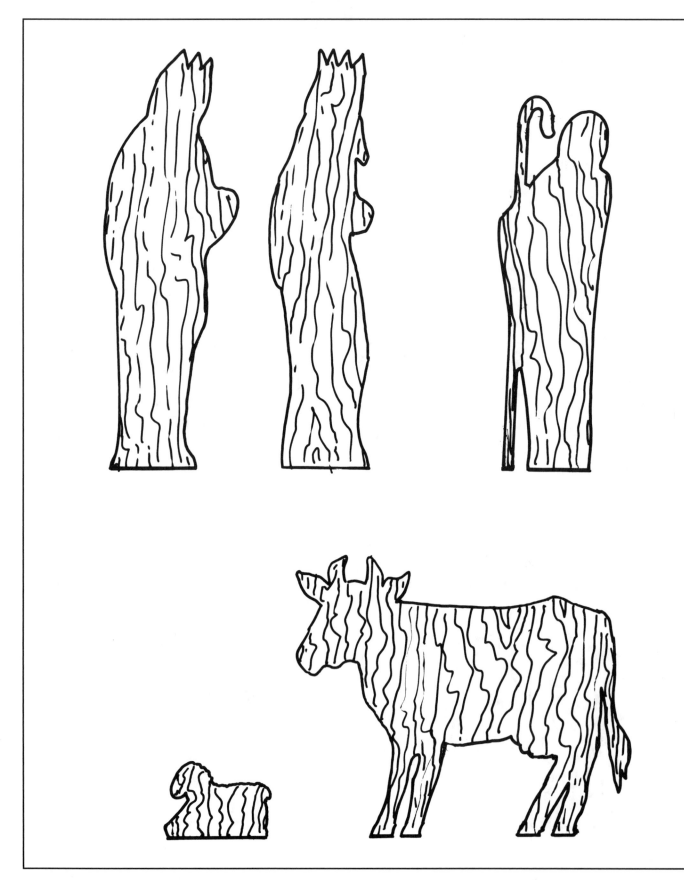

A Christmas Village

A village display as large and detailed as this would easily cost more than $100 in a shop, and the buildings would not even be hand painted. The village may be displayed all winter long; you could even change the decorations and use it all year.

MATERIALS:

3/4-inch scrap wood, paint, walnut stain, quick-drying metallic brass enamel, varnish.

TOOLS:

Scroll saw.

METHOD:

1. Transfer patterns to wood. (It's not hard to make more than one village at a time.)
2. Cut out each building; sand lightly.
3. Transfer details to each building freehand or by tracing.
4. Paint each as illustrated or as desired. (I used artist acrylic paints.) Pick colors appropriate for older buildings such as brick red, antique white, tan, brown, or liberty blue. Use quick-drying brass enamel for bell in steeple.
5. Outline windows, doors in black.
6. If you do not wish to hand paint buildings, use stencils.
7. For a Christmas village, paint candles in some windows, wreaths on doors, and snow on roofs and bushes.
8. After all buildings are dry, rub walnut stain over all surfaces and immediately rub off. This will give an antique look.
9. When dry, finish with clear satin varnish.

155

Merry Christmas

This sign can be made as large or small as you need.

MATERIALS:
3/4-inch wood, artist acrylic paint, quick-drying metallic brass enamel, varnish.

TOOLS:
Scroll saw, drill.

METHOD:
1. Lay out full-size pattern.
2. Transfer pattern to wood.
3. Cut out and sand lightly. (Best to make all interior cuts first).
4. Paint letters red, making sure to cover all corners. Use a tiny, thin brush to get into small areas.
5. When dry, paint front of letters antique white.
6. When dry, use wooden end of brush to dab 4 green dots in upper and lower corners of each letter.
7. Apply brass enamel to middle of white in each letter. The letters will wind up gold outlined in white and edged in red.
8. Finish with clear satin varnish.

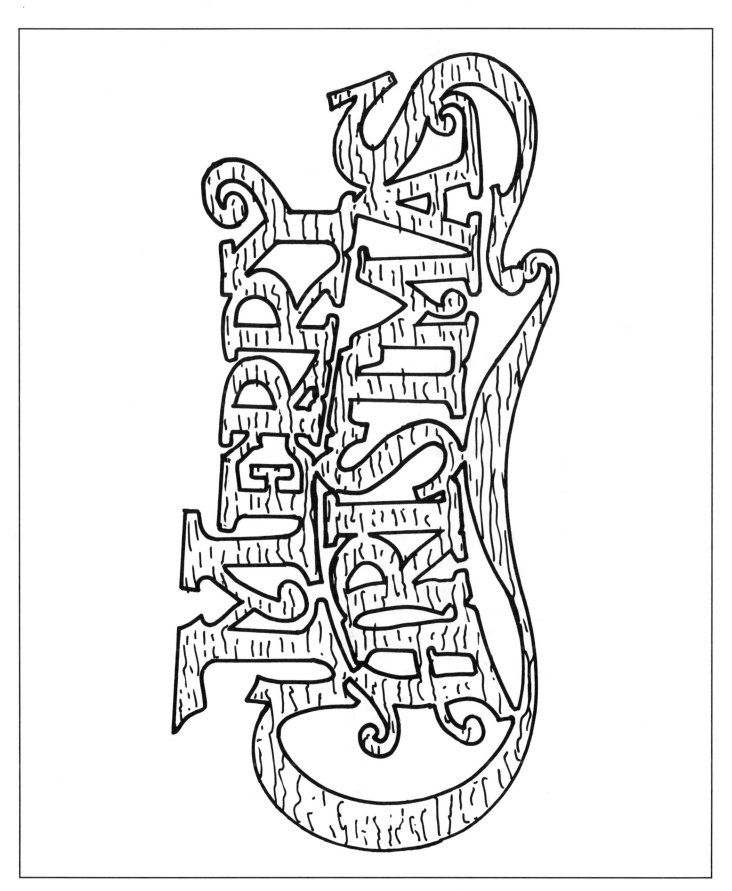

Wooden Cone Centerpiece

This is a traditional decoration used in America 150 years ago. You will need a lathe to make it. It can hold apples, pears, a pineapple, pine greens, or whatever you wish for any season.

MATERIALS:
Block of wood (soft or hard) about 4½ inches square by 14 inches long. (Glue up, if necessary, from ¾-inch-thick stock), seventy-two 6-penny nails, (8-penny if you will be hanging larger fruit), paint.

TOOLS:
Lathe, hammer, drill.

METHOD:
1. Mount block of wood on lathe and turn to approximate size noted (this is not critical). Taper as shown.
2. Paint green.
3. Add nails as shown.

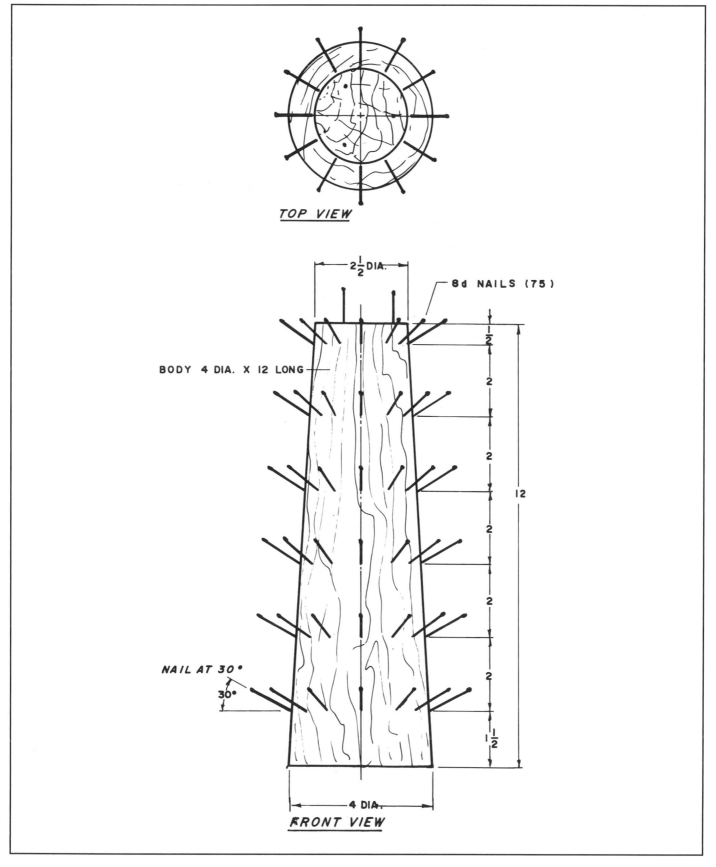

TOP VIEW

2½ DIA.

8d NAILS (75)

BODY 4 DIA. X 12 LONG

½

2

2

2

2

2

12

NAIL AT 30°

30°

1½

4 DIA.

FRONT VIEW

159

Tree with Sleigh and Merry Christmas Sign

The woodworking on this cute project is simple but it will give your painting skills a workout. Why not use it to add a festive touch to your front door?

MATERIALS:

¼-inch and ⅜-inch wood, artist acrylic paint, quick-drying metallic brass and chrome enamel paint, glue, clear gloss varnish, rubber cement.

TOOLS:

Scroll saw.

METHOD:

1. Make full-size copy of pattern.
2. Cement it to wood and cut out pieces.
3. Glue shelf to background.
4. Prime all surfaces.
5. Paint tree green, shading with blue spruce on branches.
6. Shelf and background are maroon.
7. "Merry Christmas" is metallic brass. Pinstripe around edge of sign is ivory. Snowflakes are ivory, with green snowflakes on top of ivory.
8. Sleigh is midnight blue with ivory trim and metallic silver runners trimmed with black. Packages are blue and adobe with gold and silver ribbons.
9. Reindeer are burnt umber with tail and horns white, shaded with burnt umber. Nose of deer is red and eye, black.
10. Apply clear gloss varnish.
11. Affix sleigh, reindeer to tree with wood glue.
12. If desired, affix hanger on back of the tree at top.

160

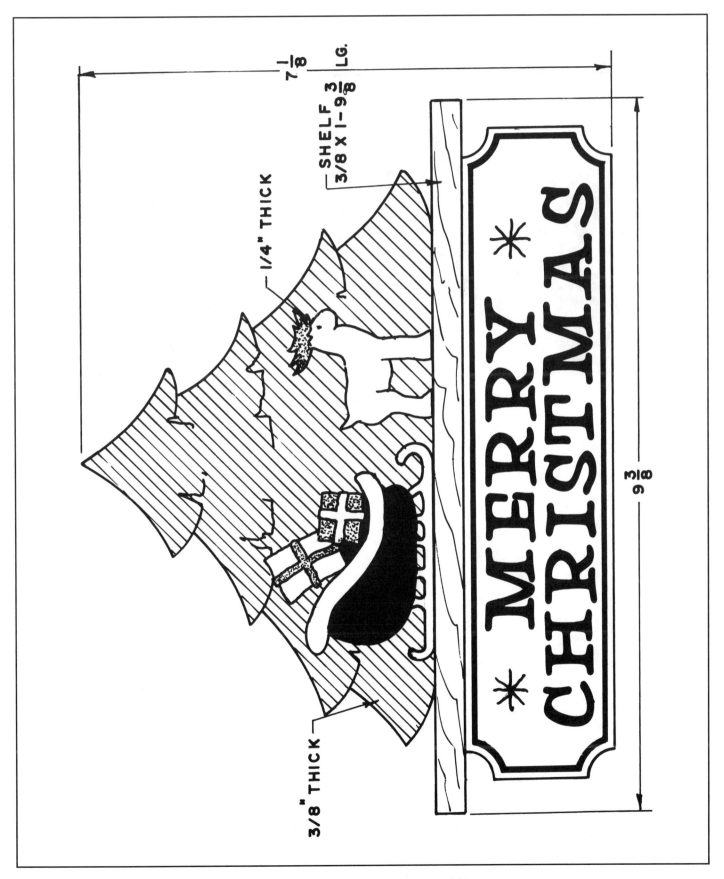

7 1/8

SHELF 3/8 X 1-9 3/8 LG.

1/4" THICK

3/8" THICK

9 3/8

MERRY CHRISTMAS

Trio of Christmas Trees

At first, my husband didn't think that this project would work out because of the compound cut described below, but in the end, it is one of his favorites.

MATERIALS:

Pine blocks (size of trees), artist acrylic paint, quick-drying metallic brass enamel, masking tape, varnish.

TOOLS:

Band saw.

METHOD:

1. Lay out full-size patterns of tree or trees you wish to make.
2. Transfer pattern to one surface of wood.
3. Using band saw, cut out tree. Save scraps.
4. Tape cut-off pieces back onto the block.
5. Turn block 90 degrees and transfer pattern to wood. Line it up with first cut.
6. Cut out and remove all tape.
7. Paint tree Christmas green.
8. Pencil in evenly spaced lines around each tree for garlands. (Small tree has 5 garlands, medium tree has 6 garlands, and large tree has 7). Paint curved strokes around pencil lines with brass enamel to create garlands.
9. When dry, paint bulbs on trees (dab paint with wooden end of brush onto trees). Use various colors, but paint one color of bulb onto all trees at once until you have desired effect.
10. When dry, finish with clear satin varnish.

162

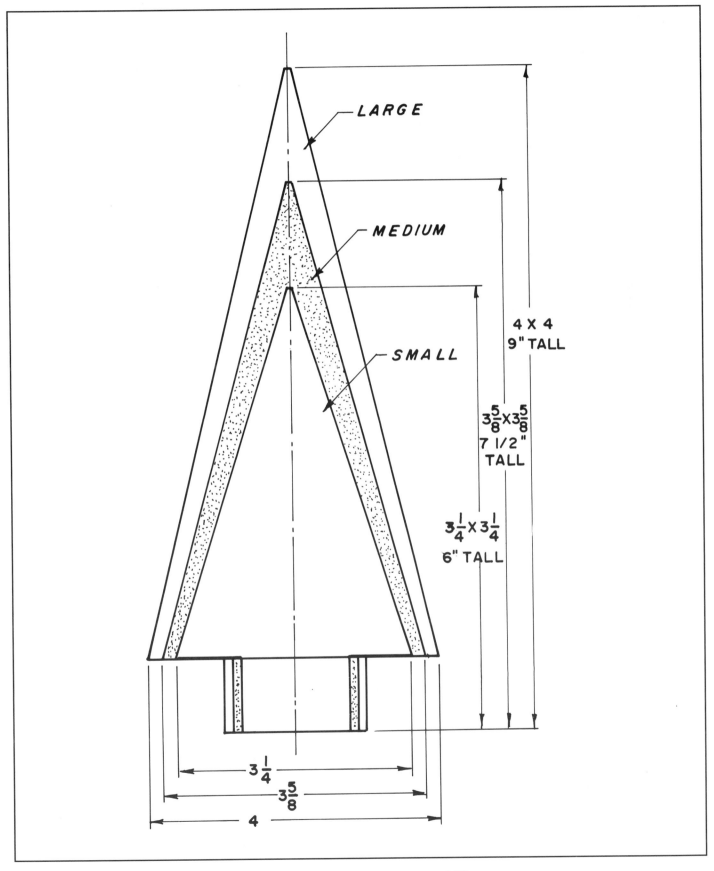

LARGE

MEDIUM

SMALL

4 X 4
9" TALL

$3\frac{5}{8}$ X $3\frac{5}{8}$
7 1/2"
TALL

$3\frac{1}{4}$ X $3\frac{1}{4}$
6" TALL

$3\frac{1}{4}$

$3\frac{5}{8}$

4

Birthday Candle Holder Numbers

This is a project you may use many times throughout the year, so it can save you some money every birthday. Just insert a few candles into the holders.

MATERIALS:
Scrap wood, small dowel, non-toxic paint.

TOOLS:
Scroll saw, drill.

METHOD:
1. Make a full-size copy of number patterns.
2. Transfer pattern to wood.
3. Drill holes for candle and peg before cutting out numbers.
4. Cut out numbers.
5. Cut pegs and glue into numbers.
6. Paint bright colors. Edges should be one color and front and back a contrasting color.
7. Sand lightly and varnish.

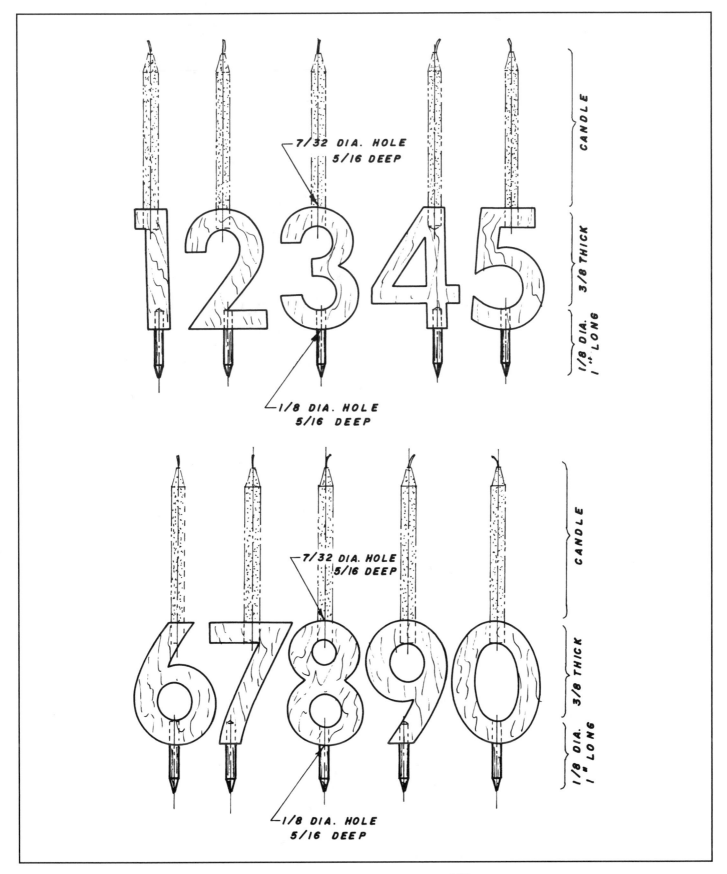

165

Sponge-Painted Pitcher and Bowl

In days past, bedrooms had a pitcher and bowl set on a nightstand for washing and drinking. This wood replication is a homey sign of your hospitality. Add plants or dry flowers for a beautiful decoration.

MATERIALS:
1/2-inch pine, sandpaper, sponge, acrylic enamel paint, stain varnish, finishing nails.

TOOLS:
Band or scroll saw, hammer, drill.

METHOD:
1. Lay out front and back pieces on heavy paper using a 1-inch grid.
2. Transfer pattern to wood.
3. Cut out pieces and sand all surfaces. Note that ends of 2 side pieces and bottom are cut at 15 degrees.
4. Assemble with finishing nails (glue optional).
5. Prime and sand lightly.
6. Paint Navajo white.
7. Sponge paint with patriot blue.
8. When dry, apply clear satin varnish.

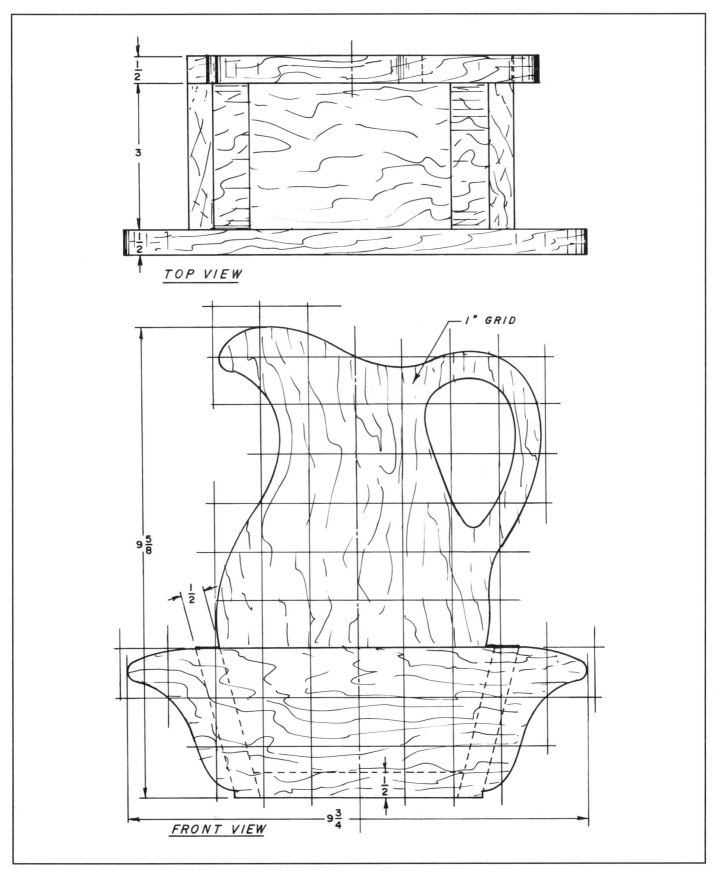

TOP VIEW

1" GRID

FRONT VIEW

$9\frac{5}{8}$

$9\frac{3}{4}$

$\frac{1}{2}$

$\frac{1}{2}$

$\frac{1}{2}$

$\frac{1}{2}$

3

$\frac{1}{2}$

Silhouette Planter

This Victorian pattern looks especially good mounted on a wall and holding ivy. Scroll saw fans will love cutting it out.

MATERIALS:

¼-inch plywood, small brads, paint, varnish.

TOOLS:

Scroll saw, drill, hammer.

METHOD:

1. Make full-size copy of patterns and glue them to plywood.
2. Carefully cut out with a fine blade. Check diameter of pot you plan to use and cut hole to fit; same goes for small brace piece. Make shelf to fit pot. Sand all surfaces.
3. Glue and nail parts together. Check that pot fits.
4. Prime. When dry, cover with black paint.
5. Sand lightly and apply clear varnish.

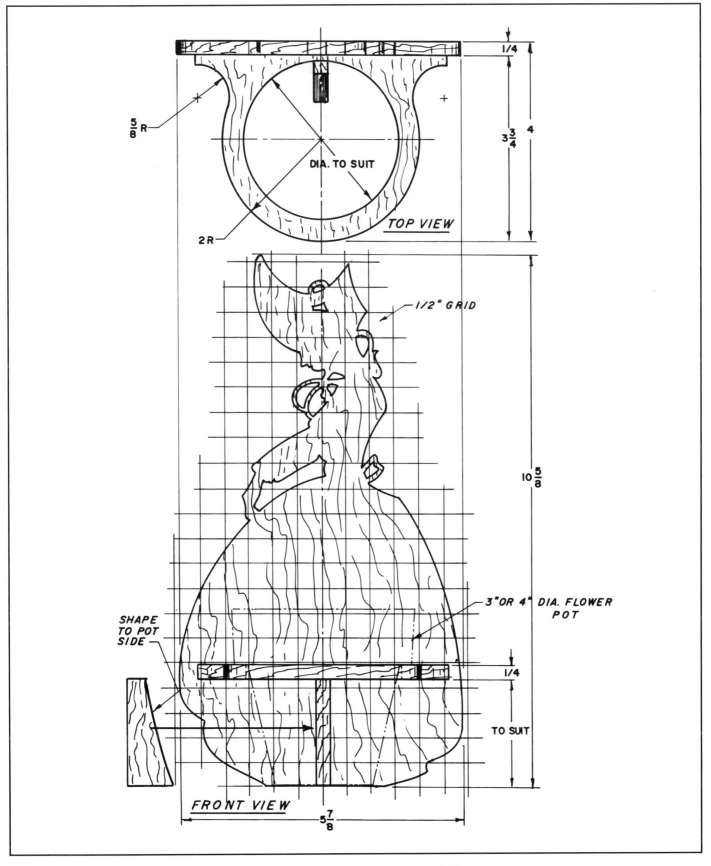

TOP VIEW

$\frac{5}{8}$R

2R

DIA. TO SUIT

1/4

$3\frac{3}{4}$ 4

1/2" GRID

$10\frac{5}{8}$

3" OR 4" DIA. FLOWER POT

SHAPE
TO POT
SIDE

1/4

TO SUIT

FRONT VIEW

$5\frac{7}{8}$

Swan Plant Holder

It's hard to beat this unusual holder for putting your favorite plant on a pedestal. It makes an impressive centerpiece.

MATERIALS:

3/4-inch pine, sandpaper, paint, walnut stain, finishing nails, satin varnish.

TOOLS:

Band or scroll saw, hammer.

METHOD:

1. Transfer pattern to wood. Grain must parallel neck as shown.
2. Stack pieces of wood and cut all 4 heads out at same time. Sand all surfaces.
3. Draw 6½-inch circle on piece of wood and cut out.
4. Nail heads together at 90 degrees, overlapping as shown in top view.
5. Center shelf and nail.
6. Prime and paint with antique white.
7. Paint beak black.
8. When dry, apply light coat of walnut stain for an antique finish.
9. Apply top coat of clear satin varnish.

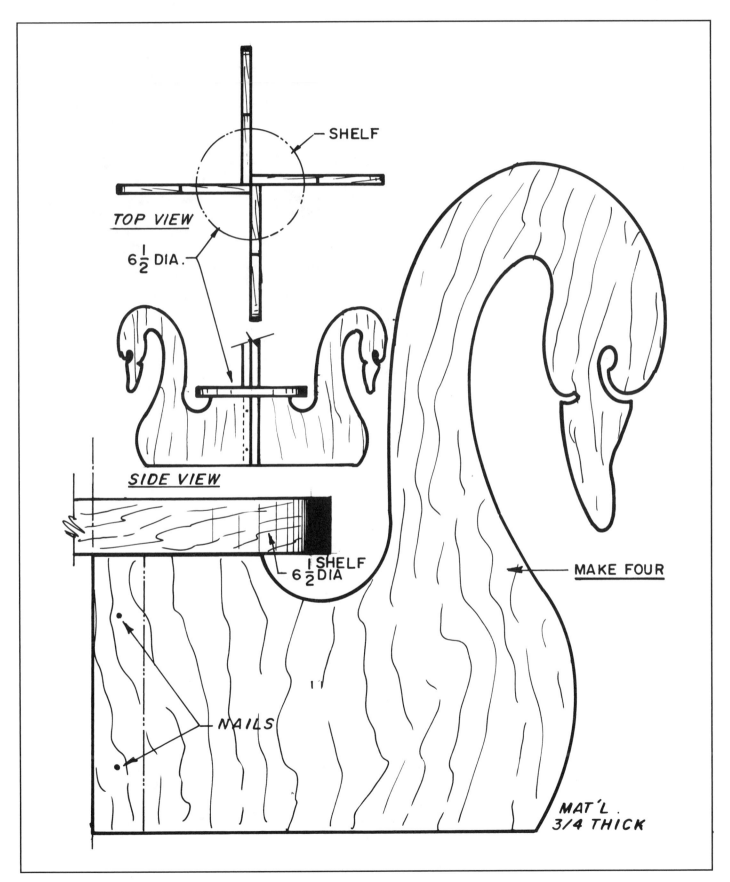

SHELF

TOP VIEW

$6\frac{1}{2}$ DIA.

SIDE VIEW

SHELF
$6\frac{1}{2}$ DIA

NAILS

MAKE FOUR

MAT'L
3/4 THICK

Welcome Sign

Place this warm sign near the door to welcome all who enter your household or business.

MATERIALS:

Pine, primer, artist acrylic paint, vellum or heavy plastic, masking tape, stencil brush, varnish, ribbon (optional).

TOOLS:

Saber or band saw, drill, X-acto knife.

METHOD:

1. Transfer pattern to wood.
2. Cut out oval shape and sand edges.
3. Locate and drill the two $3/16$-inch holes.
4. Locate and cut out heart shape.
5. Copy sign on heavy plastic or vellum. With X-acto knife, cut out letters of "welcome" to make stencil.
6. Prime all surfaces. When dry, lightly sand.
7. Apply burgundy rose paint to front.
8. Paint edges of sign and inside of heart with a dusty mauve mixed with pink. Let dry.
9. Tape stencil to project. With a stencil brush, dab on antique white paint to stencil letters.
10. Optional: Tole-paint flowers at holes that hold ribbon. This is not shown in drawing. Use a No. 6 shader artist brush. Mix dusty mauve with pink to get main color. Load brush and, starting at one side of outside of hole, pull it toward hole on first stroke. Then continue painting petals around hole clockwise, just barely overlapping previous stroke until you have made all petals of flowers.
11. When dry, sand with fine sandpaper or No. 0000 steel wool.
12. Apply top coat of varnish.
13. Put ribbon through holes from back and knot. Apply glue to back of knots to secure them.

172

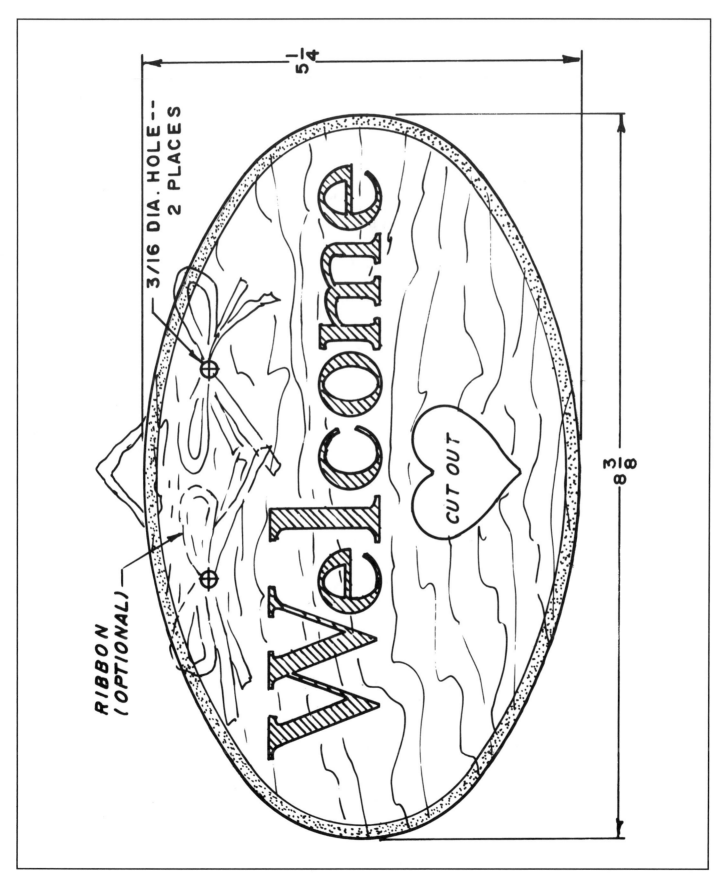

RIBBON (OPTIONAL)

3/16 DIA. HOLE — 2 PLACES

Welcome

CUT OUT

$5\frac{1}{4}$

$3\frac{3}{8}$

173

Magnets with Holiday Patterns

These 22 patterns will provide simple, quick decorations for all holidays of the year. They are reduced patterns of projects throughout the book.

MATERIALS:

Thin plywood, primer, paint, epoxy glue, small magnets, varnish.

TOOLS:

Scroll saw, sandpaper.

METHOD:

1. Transfer pattern to wood.
2. Prime wood. When dry, paint to suit.
3. Add top coat of clear varnish.
4. Cut out pattern.
5. Glue magnet to back side.

Alphabet and Numbers, Block and Script

These are all-purpose. I have included 2 alphabet styles and sets of numbers that may be used as is, enlarged, or reduced and painted as desired.

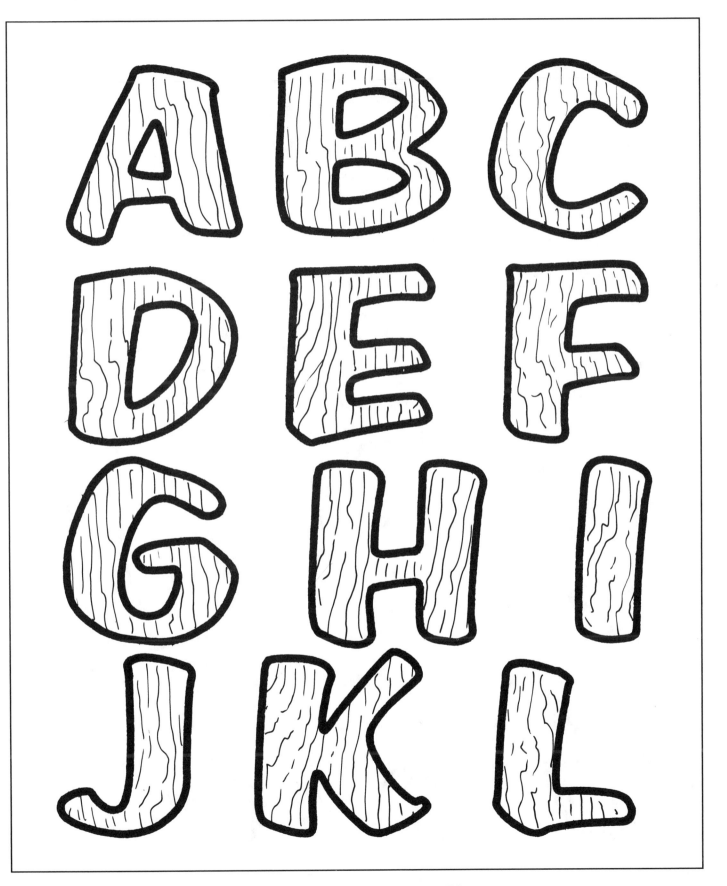

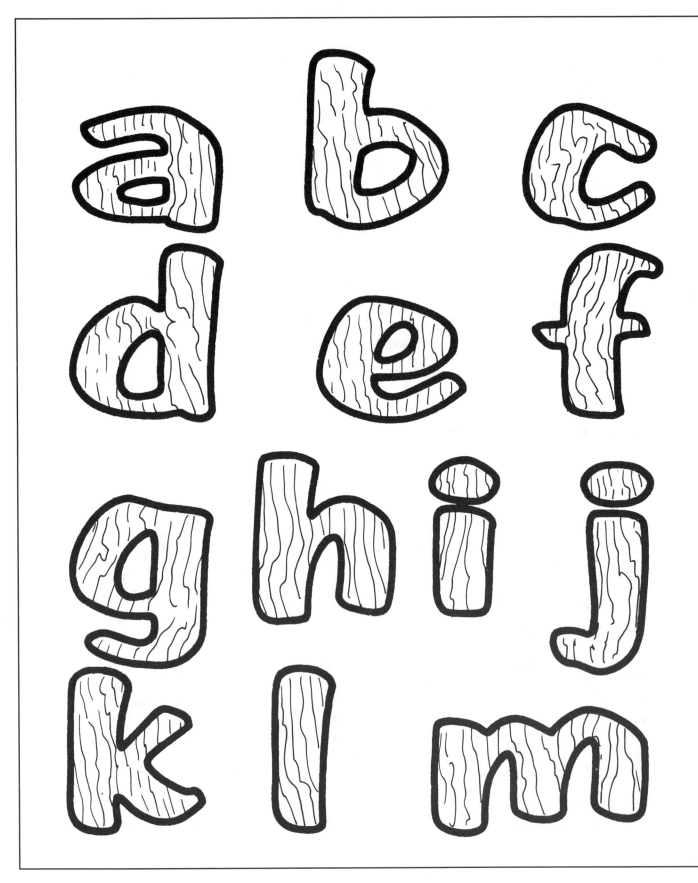

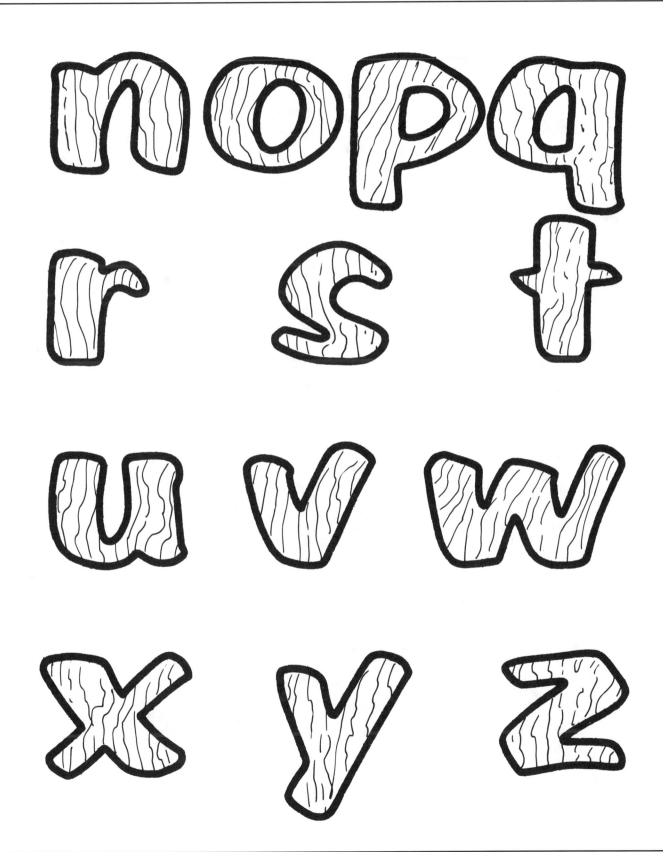

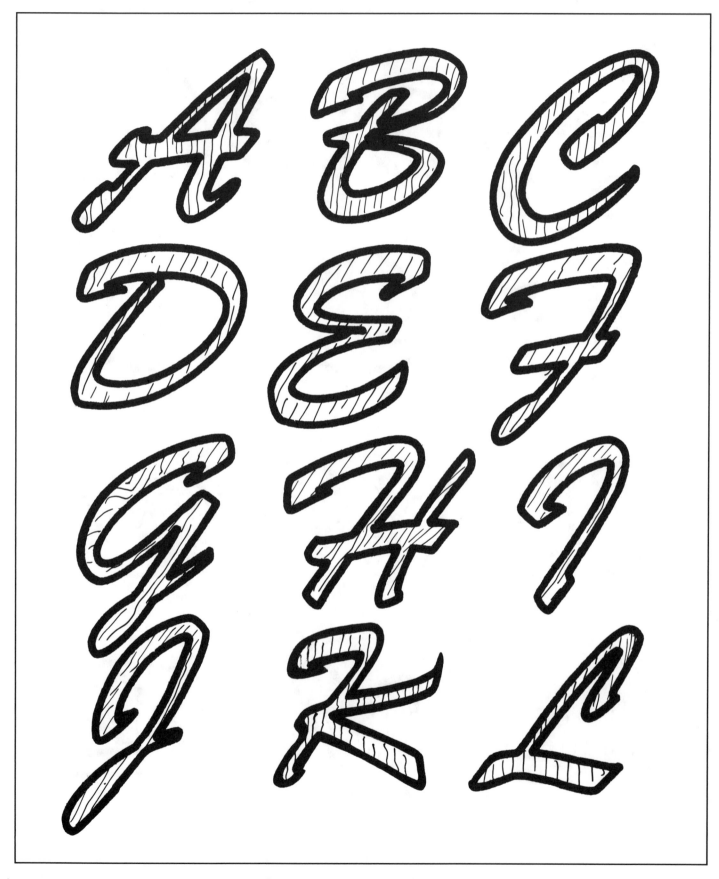

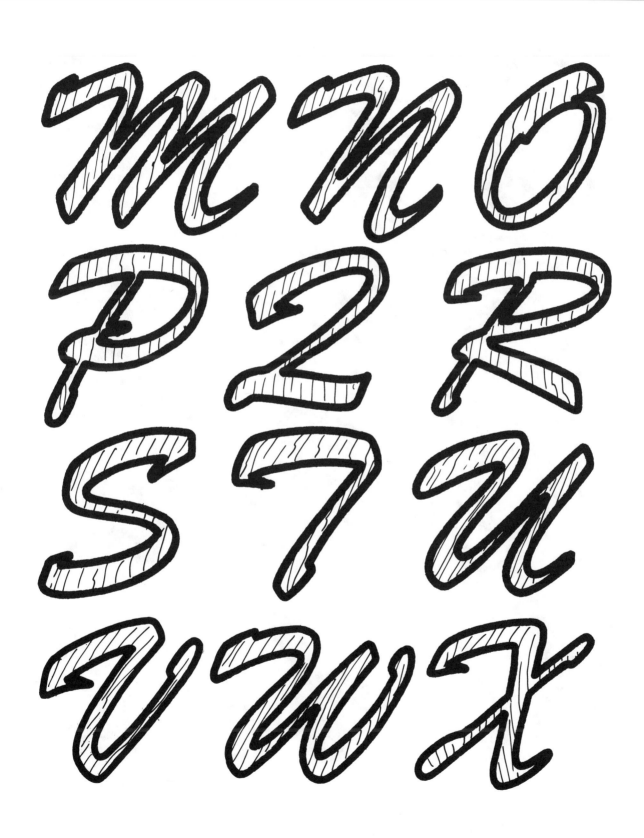

g h i j k
l m n o p
q r s t u v
w x y z

187

Suppliers

Cherry Tree Toys
P.O. Box 369
Belmont, OH 43718
(614) 484-4363

Croffwood Mills (wood only)
R.D. 1, Box 14
Driftwood, PA 15832
(800) 874-5455

Klockit (clock parts, misc.)
P.O. Box 636
Lake Geneva, WI 53147
(800) 556-2548

Leichtung Workshops
4944 Commerce Parkway
Cleveland, OH 44128
(800) 321-6840

Meisel Hardware Specialties
P.O. Box 70
Mound, MN 55364
(800) 441-9870

Rainbow Woods
20 Andrews Street
Newnan, GA 30263
(800) 423-2762

RJS Custom Woodworking
P.O. Box 12354
Kansas City, KS 66112

The Winfield Collection
1450 Torrey Road
Fenton, MI 48430-3310
(800) 927-6447

Timbers Woodworking
Timbers Building
Selma, OR 97538
(800) 762-5385

Wheelwright
(cast pewter wheels only)
3500 63rd Street
Saugatuck, MI 49453
(616) 857-1724

Woodentoy
P.O. Box 40344
Grand Junction, CO 81504